I0690539

slow cooked
PALEO

75 Real Food Recipes for
Effortless, Wholesome Meals
in Your Slow Cooker

bailey fischer

founder of Whole Kitchen Sink

PAGE STREET
PUBLISHING CO.

PAGE STREET
PUBLISHING CO.

Copyright © 2019 Bailey Fischer

First published in 2019 by Bailey Fischer
Page Street Publishing Co.
27 Congress Street, Suite 105
Salem, MA 01970
www.pagestreetpublishing.com

All rights reserved. No part of this book may be reproduced or used, in any form or by any means, electronic or mechanical, without prior permission in writing from the publisher.

Distributed by Macmillan, sales in Canada by The Canadian Manda Group.

23 22 21 20 19   1 2 3 4 5

ISBN-13: 978-1-62414-842-2
ISBN-10: 1-62414-842-5

Library of Congress Control Number: 2019930180

Cover and book design by Kylie Alexander for Page Street Publishing Co.
Photography by Bailey Fischer
Cover image by Erin Jensen

Printed and bound in China

Page Street Publishing protects our planet by donating to nonprofits like The Trustees, which focuses on local land conservation.

DEDICATION

To Justin, for always believing that my wings will work when I leap before I look, and that the bridge will manifest beneath me when I run before I'm ready. For never doubting my dreams before I've found a way to catch them, and for your patience with me in the grocery store. Thank you. For all of it. I love you.

CONTENTS

FOREWORD

It's not a big secret that cooking isn't my thing—eating is. I make no bones about the fact that I think food is meant to be enjoyed, and I refuse to waste time eating food that doesn't bring me total satisfaction. I love the aromas, the visual experience of looking at a beautifully prepared plate, the social connection that comes with sharing a meal with friends and loved ones, and of course the gustatory pleasure of eating delicious foods. These are some of the greatest joys in life.

I deeply appreciate people who share my passion for food, especially folks who also recognize that real food tastes better. By "real food" I mean meat, fish, fowl, eggs, vegetables, fruits, nuts and seeds—the items that I have been urging people to eat for over a decade on my blog, Mark's Daily Apple. These are the foods that have nourished us for all of human history; the foods that send epigenetic signals for health, longevity and vitality to every one of the cells in our bodies; the foods that connect us back to farmers and ranchers and the land itself.

Bailey shares my passion and my belief that food should be as delicious and as nutritious as possible. She gets it. Her recipes are exactly how I like to eat: simple to prepare, flavorful food made with quality ingredients. She is welcome to come to my home and make my wife Carrie and I some Better-For-You Beef Bourguignon (page 74) or Butternut-Bacon Bisque with Shrimp (page 119) anytime!

Of course, I'm honored that she chose to feature my Primal Kitchen condiments in this book. The easiest way to elevate simple food preparations is to add sauces and dressings that take them to the next level. Making basic ingredients like meat and vegetables taste amazing is easy when you have access to healthy condiments. And when you have recipes like Bailey's that give you fresh ideas for how to use them, that's a win-win.

I am always working toward making healthy food options exciting and accessible for everyone. Bailey has taken the same approach with the recipes in this book. Too often, people are afraid to make the leap to Paleo/Primal (or just "healthy") diets because they are afraid that eating this way is difficult, time-consuming and burdensome. Or, they believe that healthy food is boring and bland. The more people we have like Bailey—showing people that it's not only possible, but simple to make tasty, healthful food—the better. No excuses now!

So, thank you for picking up a copy of *Slow Cooked Paleo*. I have dedicated the last two decades to educating people about how eating well is a cornerstone of every aspect of health and longevity. I want to thank Bailey for continuing to spread this message on her blog, Whole Kitchen Sink, and with this book. Bailey is one of the ambassadors for the Paleo/Primal lifestyle who make a tremendous difference in stemming the tide of modern, preventable chronic illnesses and promoting a better way forward. I am happy to support her in continuing to bring Paleo to the masses. Keep it up, Bailey!

Mark Sisson

INTRODUCTION

Transitioning to the Paleo diet can seem overwhelming, but with this collection of easy, flavor-packed recipes and the help of your slow cooker, the process is effortless—and even outright enjoyable! The slow cooker has so many benefits beyond doing the majority of the cooking for you. I chose to focus on healthy, wholesome meals made in the slow cooker because of the diverse yet approachable array of nutritious, budget-friendly recipes that can be made in one easy appliance. Many of the dishes you'll find here are Paleo takes on classic favorites, which helps make it smoother to transition to a real-food diet without giving up the flavor and familiarity of the dishes you know and love. These recipes will show you how easy it can be to get a healthy Paleo dinner on the table, and how they can be tailored to suit many other dietary needs, such as low carb, autoimmune protocol (AIP), vegan or vegetarian, so everyone can find something they're looking for.

The health benefits of eating Paleo by introducing more real foods into your diet and cutting out the processed ones are numerous (and incredible, if you ask me). You're bound to find yourself with increased energy, sounder sleep, a sharper mind, better performance in your workouts and even down a few pounds. The old adage is true . . . you really should eat your vegetables, and these recipes will help you do it!

Utilizing the slow cooker for your Paleo lifestyle can also do your budget a lot of favors. This was an important factor in the recipes in this book. Not only do I keep your wallet in mind, but I also make eating a real-food diet easier for you and your family for the long haul—even if it means working in less-expensive cuts of meat a few nights a week to balance out the cost of other items like almond flour, coconut aminos and the more expensive almond butter without added sugar.

I know all too well how hard it can be to prioritize your health, work toward weight loss if that's a goal or transition away from gluten, dairy, grain and soy. But I also know it can be done. This book is exactly what I needed when I began my own weight loss journey with Paleo but didn't know how to cook for myself, and then when I realized how great eating real food made me feel but was overwhelmed balancing time in the kitchen with my 12-hour overnight shifts. My hope is that you use these recipes to find better health and that you see how capable you are of making the Paleo diet an attainable, delicious, everyday part of your life.

With love, and in health,
Bailey

♡ Bailey Fischer

SLOW COOKER TIPS, TRICKS, DOS AND DON'TS

My go-to slow cooker is a basic 6-quart (5.4-L) model with the no-frills setting options of high, low and keep warm. This capacity is large enough to make generous helpings for a family dinner or for meal prepping, and it's just the right size to fit roasts, stews and egg bakes without overfilling. The recipes in this book have been developed with the 6-quart (5.4-L) slow cooker in mind, unless otherwise noted. Most recipes intended for a 6-quart (5.4-L) model will still work just fine in a 7- or an 8-quart (6.3- or 7.2-L) model, although the cook time will be slightly altered.

When using a smaller model for the recipes meant for the standard 6-quart (5.4-L) size, such as a 4-quart (3.6-L) slow cooker, you can either reduce the quantity of ingredients or reduce the liquid required, depending on the recipe. The opposite applies to recipes, such as ones found in the dessert section, that call for a 2- or 3-quart (1.8- or 2.7-L) slow cooker. You can scale up the recipe to fit your slow cooker by doubling or tripling the ingredients and increasing the cook time.

Next, get to know your slow cooker! There are so many models out there nowadays, and only you know best how yours works. Some slow cookers run hot and some have "hot spots" on one of the sides. Cooking temperatures can range drastically between models, with one model's cooking temperature on high being 210°F (99°C) and another's being 300°F (149°C). Nuances in individual cookers will affect how much time is needed and cooking times can fall on the low or high end of the wide cooking time ranges that are given with slow cooker recipes.

Avoid removing the lid as much as possible to peek or stir if it's not needed. I know it's tempting when your home starts smelling incredible, but every time the lid is opened and all of that heat escapes, it takes about 25 minutes for the slow cooker to reach the set temperature again.

Another helpful tip is to make sure you slice, chop and dice vegetables and meat into equal sizes. While it doesn't have to be an exact science, cutting up things like root veggies into the same size means that you won't have some pieces undercooked and others overcooked in the same dish.

Don't overdo it on the liquids. The liquid that's released from the food remains in the slow cooker and continues to baste the food instead of evaporating. Adding too much liquid can create an unintended soup instead, so hold off and if you want more liquid for a gravy, or for your meal, it's easy to add at the end.

On the flip side, if you have too much liquid at the end, you can get rid of the excess by venting the slow cooker. Simply tilt the slow cooker lid off center a bit to create an opening for the steam to escape, and turn the cooker to low if it isn't already. Thirty minutes to an hour will thicken any liquidy dish.

You'll see instructions to thicken sauces or soups by using a slurry of equal parts arrowroot flour and water. Tapioca flour can always be used in these recipes instead of arrowroot. Depending on how much liquid the vegetables and meat release during cooking, additional arrowroot may be needed to achieve your desired thickness. Add an extra ½ tablespoon (4 g) until the sauce is thickened to your liking.

If you choose to start off your slow cooker dish with frozen meat, you'll need to adjust the cooking time to compensate. In most cases, such as soups, this is a fine option, but there are some recipes that you may want to just thaw the meat first to ensure it cooks correctly. Allow for an additional 4 hours on low or 2 hours on high if you're using frozen meat.

CHAPTER 1

Effortless MORNING MEALS

It wasn't long ago that I was struggling to figure out Paleo breakfast meals that I enjoyed *and* that were easy. After spending more than two decades grabbing a frosted toaster pastry or sweet cereal bar on my way out the door, getting drive-thru or skipping it altogether, creating a new routine that included vegetables during already-rushed mornings felt impossible. Soon it seemed like I'd been doing it forever once I began batch cooking breakfasts, prepping real-food options that were still grab-and-go such as Savory Breakfast Sausage Meatballs (page 33) and Chicken Fajita Breakfast Casserole (page 21) and making sure I had individual portions of my favorite egg bake in the freezer ready to get reheated on a moment's notice.

I hope these recipes will make it easier to fit in a real-food breakfast that fuels your day, or that they bring your family around the table on a slow Saturday morning to share a nourishing meal. After all, eating Paleo becomes so much more sustainable when it works *with* you and your life instead of against it!

EGGS IN
SLOW PURGATORY

There's no shortage of tasty variations for this easy and healthy meal, and many cultures have their own traditional version of it. Each one reflects the unique culture it was born from, and it's a wonderful example of how food unites us all.

Eggs in purgatory are typically started on the stovetop and finished in the oven, but in my variation, I love the deep flavor that's created by the tomato sauce and spices simmering and melding together. It's also much easier to clean up when it's all contained in the slow cooker, unlike how messy simmering tomato sauce on the stovetop can get!

1 (28-oz [784-g]) can whole plum tomatoes, chopped and with liquid

1 medium red onion, thinly sliced

1 red bell pepper, cored and sliced

1 green bell pepper, cored and sliced

1 tbsp (10 g) minced garlic

1 cup (150 g) cherry tomatoes, halved

½ cup (30 g) loosely packed chopped Italian parsley

2 tsp (5 g) ground cumin

2 tsp (5 g) smoked paprika

1 tsp dried basil

1 tsp dried oregano

½ tsp salt

¼ tsp ground black pepper

½ cup (30 g) loosely packed fresh dill (optional)

4 eggs

Fresh herbs, for garnish

Add the canned tomatoes, onion, bell peppers, garlic, cherry tomatoes, parsley, cumin, paprika, basil, oregano, salt, pepper and dill, if using, to the slow cooker and stir well to combine. Cover and cook on low for 2 to 4 hours, or on high for 1 to 2 hours.

Once the tomatoes and vegetables have cooked down into a thick, chunky sauce, use an immersion blender to blend in the slow cooker until it's the texture you prefer. Or leave as is for a chunkier tomato sauce.

Next, create wells in the sauce with a spoon. Gently crack an egg into a measuring cup and pour into the well. Do this for each egg, leaving a bit of space between the eggs. Turn the slow cooker to low, cover and let the eggs cook for 15 minutes or more, depending on how well done you like your yolks. Garnish with fresh herbs before serving.

COOKING TIP:

- *Use diced tomatoes instead of whole tomatoes if you don't have an immersion blender or just want a thinner sauce.*

Per serving: Calories: 158 | Fat: 5 g | Carbs: 16.8 g | Fiber: 5.6 g | Protein: 9.4 g

JUSTIN'S BACON BREAKFAST PIE

This egg bake is named after the person I make it for most: my husband Justin. It's made almost weekly in our house because it's an easy, hands-free way to prepare breakfasts for the week, without me needing to pay attention to my oven. This breakfast pie is also great to feed guests or to make during holidays. If you're not an early riser, you can cook the meat and prep the rest of the recipe the night before and start it in the morning with your eyes still shut!

SERVES 6

1 lb (455 g) hash browns or grated potatoes, thawed if frozen

1 red bell pepper, cored and diced (about 1 cup [150 g])

1 green bell pepper, cored and diced (about 1 cup [150 g])

1 medium white onion, diced (about 1 cup [150 g])

12 eggs

⅓ cup (80 g) canned coconut milk (solid part)

1 tsp salt

½ tsp ground black pepper

12 slices (about 12 oz [340 g]) sugar-free bacon, cooked and chopped, plus more for garnish

Sliced green onions, for garnish

Line the slow cooker with parchment paper or coat the insert with oil. Combine the hash browns, bell peppers and onion in a bowl and add to the slow cooker.

In a large bowl, beat the eggs with the coconut milk, salt and pepper. Mix in the bacon and stir into the slow cooker over the vegetables. Cook on high for 2 to 2½ hours, or until the eggs have set in the middle. Try to open the lid as little as possible during the cook time. Garnish with the green onions and more bacon before serving.

To freeze, remove the breakfast pie from the slow cooker using the parchment paper and allow to completely cool. You can freeze the entire breakfast pie or cut it into serving sizes and freeze as individual servings. Store in the freezer for up to 3 months. Thaw in the refrigerator overnight, or up to 24 hours. Reheat in the microwave or in the oven.

COOKING TIPS:

- *Omit the hash browns to make this low carb. Use almond milk to make this coconut-free.*

- *Use chip clips around the rim of the slow cooker insert to hold the parchment paper in place while preparing the recipe.*

Per serving: Calories: 301 | Fat: 15.3 g | Carbs: 17.2 g | Fiber: 2.9 g | Protein: 19 g

SLOW SUNRISE HASH

Hash has always been one of my favorite breakfasts, especially when I've had my fill of eggs for the week. Hash is easy to make, is a great "clean out the fridge" meal to use up random vegetables and reduce food waste and tastes great as leftovers too! Add or replace any vegetables you prefer or want to use up. Vegetables with a longer cook time, such as squash, should be added first, and vegetables that cook quickly, such as zucchini, should be added in the last 30 minutes. You can also incorporate sliced breakfast sausage, kielbasa or chopped bacon for a non-vegetarian option.

NUT-FREE · VEGETARIAN · LOW-CARB OPTION · EGG-FREE · AIP FRIENDLY OPTION (AIP)

SERVES 4

2 cups (280 g) peeled and cubed butternut squash

2 cups (180 g) halved or quartered Brussels sprouts

1½ tbsp (22 ml) avocado oil, divided

1 clove garlic, minced

Juice of ½ lemon, plus more for serving

1 tsp dried rosemary, plus more for serving

¼ tsp smoked paprika

Salt and ground black pepper, to taste

1 small zucchini, sliced

1 cup (150 g) halved cherry tomatoes

1 cup (30 g) baby spinach

Chopped avocado, for serving (optional)

Place the squash, Brussels sprouts, 1 tablespoon (15 ml) of the oil, garlic, lemon juice, rosemary, paprika, salt and pepper into the slow cooker. Stir to combine and cover. Cook on low for 3 to 4 hours or on high for 1 to 2 hours, until the butternut squash is fork-tender.

Mix in the zucchini, tomatoes and spinach. Add the remaining ½ tablespoon (7 ml) of oil if needed. Cover and cook on low for an additional 30 minutes, or until the zucchini is fork-tender and the spinach has wilted. Top with more rosemary, fresh lemon juice or chopped avocado, if desired.

COOKING TIP:

- *Swap out the tomatoes and omit the paprika for AIP.*

Per serving: Calories: 101 | Fat: 4.2 g | Carbs: 12.6 g | Fiber: 4.6 g | Protein: 2.9 g

CHICKEN FAJITA BREAKFAST CASSEROLE

This recipe is a far cry from the drive-thru breakfast order I used to get from the Mexican fast food restaurant on my way home from a 12-hour overnight shift. I may have ditched that habit, but my love of chicken fajitas turned breakfast food hasn't changed. This recipe takes those favorite flavors and drops them into a delicious Paleo casserole that's much healthier but still quick and easy. It's a great recipe to use up leftover chicken or change up your usual breakfast routine. If you want to really spice up this recipe, mix a diced jalapeño or a few dashes of cayenne pepper or hot sauce into the eggs.

SERVES 6

3 grain-free tortillas (optional)

10 eggs

½ cup (120 ml) almond milk or coconut milk

2 cups (250 g) shredded chicken

1 cup (150 g) diced red onion

1 cup (150 g) diced red bell pepper

1 (4-oz [112-g]) can diced green chiles

2 tsp (5 g) chili powder

1 tsp cumin

1 tsp salt

½ tsp ground black pepper

GARNISHES (OPTIONAL)

Salsa, homemade (page 172) or store-bought

Hot sauce

Chopped cilantro

Chopped avocado

Line the slow cooker with parchment paper or coat the insert with nonstick cooking spray. If you're using grain-free tortillas, layer them on the bottom and up the sides about 2 inches (5 cm).

In a large bowl, beat the eggs and then mix in the dairy-free milk, chicken, onion, pepper, chiles, chili powder, cumin, salt and pepper.

Pour the egg and vegetable mixture into the slow cooker and cook on low for 2 to 3 hours, or until the eggs are set. Top with the optional garnishes.

To freeze, remove the casserole from the slow cooker using the parchment paper and allow to completely cool. You can freeze the entire casserole or cut it into serving sizes and freeze as individual servings. Store in the freezer for up to 3 months. Thaw in the refrigerator overnight, or up to 24 hours. Reheat in the microwave or the oven.

COOKING TIPS:

- *For a fun variation, mix 1 cup (240 ml) of salsa with the beaten eggs and increase the cook time by approximately 30 minutes.*

- *Use chip clips around the rim of the slow cooker insert to hold the parchment paper in place while preparing the recipe.*

Per serving: Calories: 340 | Fat: 17.1 g | Carbs: 9.1 g | Fiber: 1.6 g | Protein: 33.8 g

HOMEMADE COCONUT YOGURT

Yogurt is one of the easiest and most economical recipes you can make in your slow cooker. The small containers of store-bought dairy-free yogurt can get expensive, and it's something that I have a hard time justifying as a regular purchase. Making it right on your own kitchen counter cuts costs and is still rich in probiotics and great for digestive health. It can take some time to ferment, but with a little bit of patience, this recipe basically makes itself. Using the right coconut milk is key for the creamiest, best-tasting results. Make sure you're using full-fat coconut milk that consists of only coconut and water.

MAKES SEVEN ½-CUP (120-G) SERVINGS

2 (13.5-oz [378-ml]) cans full-fat coconut milk

¼ cup (60 g) coconut or almond yogurt with live cultures (dairy or soy yogurt has the same effect as well)

1 tbsp (7 g) gelatin

Make sure all of the dishes the yogurt will be touching are extremely clean. Running the slow cooker and whisk under extremely hot water or using the "sanitize" option on a dishwasher, if available, works best.

In a 2- to 4-quart (1.8- to 3.6-L) slow cooker, add the coconut milk and cook on low for 2½ to 3 hours. Turn the slow cooker off, keep covered and let sit for 3 hours to cool. The milk should still be warm, but not hot enough to kill the live bacteria.

Next, stir in the yogurt and gelatin. Cover again and use a thick towel that blocks light to cover the slow cooker and set aside to ferment for 12 to 24 hours. The longer you let it ferment, up to 36 hours, the thicker the yogurt will be.

Once it's done, store it in the fridge for up to 10 days. Keep in mind that the yogurt will continue to thicken and become more tart over time in the refrigerator.

COOKING TIPS:

- *Make flavored yogurt by stirring in 1 to 2 tablespoons (15 to 30 ml) of vanilla extract and 1 tablespoon (15 to 20 ml) of your sweetener of choice, such as maple syrup or honey.*

- *You can also use a store-bought yogurt starter culture. Make sure to reserve ¼ to ½ cup (60 to 120 g) from your first batch to use as a yogurt starter next time.*

- *If you want to use your own probiotic capsules, use 2 to 3 capsules per each can of coconut milk. Be aware that the taste, texture and overall result of the yogurt will vary depending on the type of probiotic you use.*

Per serving: Calories: 195 | Fat: 18.9 g | Carbs: 1.7 g | Fiber: 0 g | Protein: 3.3 g

FARMER'S BREAKFAST

Farmer's breakfast is a name that's generally used to describe breakfasts that are quick and have enough carbs and protein to keep that hardworking farmer going strong through the day. This is such a hearty and filling Paleo meal to prep ahead for the week or to feed the family. This breakfast is easy to customize by adding your favorite spices or sausage or topping it with an egg just before eating. Pair with hard-boiled eggs if prepping for the week ahead.

SERVES 6

12–16 oz (340–455 g) sugar-free breakfast sausage links (Pederson's, Applegate or Aidells)

4 cups (600 g) diced gold potatoes

2 long carrots, peeled and diced (about 1 cup [150 g])

1 red bell pepper, cored and diced (about 1 cup [150 g])

1 cup (150 g) cherry tomatoes, halved

1 heaping tbsp (3 g) chopped fresh dill or 1½ tsp (2 g) dried

1 tbsp (15 ml) melted ghee, homemade (page 180) or store-bought, or avocado oil

1 tbsp (15 ml) white wine vinegar

1 tsp garlic powder

1 tsp salt

½ tsp onion powder

½ tsp ground black pepper

FOR SERVING (OPTIONAL)

Eggs

Diced green onion

Hot sauce

Salsa, homemade (page 172) or store-bought

First, if you desire crispier sausages, heat a skillet over medium heat and sear the sausages for 2 minutes on each side. Remove from the heat.

Add the potatoes, carrots, bell pepper, tomatoes, dill, ghee, vinegar, garlic powder, salt, onion powder and black pepper to the slow cooker. Stir to evenly coat the vegetables with the spices and ghee.

Place the sausages on top of the vegetables and cover the slow cooker. Cook on low for 5 to 6 hours, or on high for 2½ to 3 hours.

Prior to serving, cook any eggs you may want with it and top with green onion, hot sauce or salsa, if desired. Slice or leave the sausages whole.

To freeze uncooked, leave out the potatoes and then add them when you are ready to cook. If reheating the fully cooked meal from frozen, do not thaw first. Place the frozen meal directly into the preheated slow cooker or oven to keep the potatoes fresh.

COOKING TIP:

- *To make this low carb, swap the diced carrots for quartered Brussels sprouts and the diced potatoes for peeled and diced turnips.*

Per serving: Calories: 305 | Fat: 13.8 g | Carbs: 33.6 g | Fiber: 5.3 g | Protein: 12.8 g

SPINACH AND MUSHROOM CRUSTLESS QUICHE

SERVES 6

I'm always trying to come up with new combinations for our weekly slow cooker Paleo egg bakes, and many times it's Justin who gives me the ideas. Which only makes sense, given that he's the main beneficiary. This recipe was born out of a need for a meatless option that could be paired with my homemade breakfast sausages (see page 34 for my DIY spice combination) and a need to use up fresh herbs. During the process of recipe testing, I've swapped the fresh herbs for dried so you're more likely to have the spices on hand. If you have fresh oregano and parsley, use 1 tablespoon (3 g) chopped fresh herbs for every 1 teaspoon dried in the recipe.

10 eggs

¼ cup (60 ml) dairy-free milk

2 cups (140 g) sliced or diced mushrooms

2 cups (60 g) baby spinach

1 cup (150 g) finely diced red onion

2–3 green onions, white and light green parts, chopped

2 tsp (2 g) dried oregano

2 tsp (1 g) dried parsley

½ tsp salt, or to taste

¼ tsp ground black pepper, or to taste

Chopped onion or fresh parsley, for garnish (optional)

In a large mixing bowl, beat the eggs until well blended. Add the milk, mushrooms, spinach, red onion, green onions, oregano, parsley, salt and pepper. Mix well until evenly combined.

Line the slow cooker with parchment paper or coat the slow cooker insert with nonstick cooking spray, and pour the egg mixture into the slow cooker. Cook on high for 2 to 2½ hours or on low for 4 hours, or until the eggs are set in the middle. Remove using the edges of the parchment paper and cut into slices or squares. Garnish with chopped onion or fresh parsley, if desired.

To freeze, remove the egg bake from the slow cooker using the parchment paper and allow to completely cool. You can freeze the entire casserole or cut it into serving sizes and freeze as individual servings. Store in the freezer for up to 3 months. Thaw in the refrigerator overnight, or up to 24 hours. Reheat in the microwave or in the oven.

COOKING TIP:

- *Use chip clips around the rim of the slow cooker insert to hold the parchment paper in place while preparing the recipe.*

Per serving: Calories: 212 | Fat: 12.2 g | Carbs: 7.6 g | Fiber: 1.3 g | Protein: 17.2 g

DINER BREAKFAST POTATOES

Breakfast potatoes are a classic veggie to go along with your sausage or eggs. This recipe makes enough to enjoy all week, or to add to a brunch menu or serve with a holiday meal. Making them in the slow cooker doubles as an easy way to serve and keep them warm! Leftovers are fantastic to add to a quick breakfast skillet or as a dinner side paired with Simple Smothered Pork Chops (page 110), Homemade Salisbury Steak (page 83) or Pulled Peppered Beef Brisket with Onion Gravy (page 77), or served under Smoky Chorizo Chicken (page 106) or Best Ever Beef Ragu (page 88).

SERVES 8

2–3 lb (910–1350 g) red potatoes, quartered or cut into 1½" (3.8-cm) pieces

1 red bell pepper, cored and diced

1 green bell pepper, cored and diced

1 cup (150 g) diced white onion (about 1 onion)

1 tbsp (10 g) minced garlic

½ tbsp (1 g) dried parsley

1 tsp salt, plus more to taste

½ tsp ground black pepper, plus more to taste

2 tbsp (30 ml) melted ghee, homemade (page 180) or store-bought

1 tbsp (15 ml) olive oil

Chopped fresh parsley, for garnish (optional)

Coat the slow cooker insert with nonstick cooking spray. Add the potatoes, bell peppers, onion, garlic, dried parsley, salt and black pepper to the slow cooker, drizzling the ghee and olive oil over everything. Stir to combine.

Cook on low for 6 to 8 hours, or until the potatoes are fork-tender. Remove the lid and stir halfway through the cook time.

Once finished, add salt and black pepper to taste. Top with fresh parsley, if desired.

COOKING TIPS:

- *Swap the potatoes with chopped radishes or turnips for a low-carb spin.*
- *Stir in sliced kielbasa or breakfast sausage for a protein, or top with cooked and chopped bacon before serving.*

Per serving: Calories: 218 | Fat: 5.5 g | Carbs: 38 g | Fiber: 4.6 g | Protein: 12.8 g

MASON JAR FRITTATAS

These breakfast jars are perfectly portable, which makes them the ideal morning meal for your life on the go. I made these all the time when I was a student spending weekdays rushing off to an 8 a.m. class, and now we rely on them still during busy weeks to make getting out the door with a filling breakfast in hand a quick and painless process. The beauty of these frittatas is that they're entirely customizable. Add your preferred spices, any meat you already have on hand and your family's favorite vegetables to make them your own!

**MAKES FOUR
1-PINT (455-G) JARS**

2⅔ cups (400 g) thawed hash browns or grated potatoes (⅔ cup per jar)

1⅓ cups (200 g) diced butternut squash (⅓ cup per jar)

1⅓ cups (200 g) diced green bell pepper (⅓ cup per jar)

12 eggs

½ cup (120 ml) dairy-free milk, plus more to rehydrate

1 tsp salt

½ tsp ground black pepper

1 handful spinach, chopped

Evenly distribute the hash browns, squash and bell pepper among four 1-pint (455-g) Mason jars.

In a large bowl, beat the eggs with the milk, salt and black pepper and then pour into the jars. The egg should just about cover the vegetables. Top with the chopped spinach.

Transfer the jars to the slow cooker and add water to the insert until three-fourths of the jars are covered. Cover the slow cooker and cook on low for 3 to 4 hours, then turn the slow cooker to the warm setting and leave the jars for 3 more hours, or until the eggs have set.

Allow to completely cool and then cover the jars with the lids. Store in the refrigerator for up to 5 days. To reheat, remove the metal lid and microwave for 1 to 1½ minutes. Add 1 or 2 tablespoons (15 to 30 ml) of dairy-free milk to the jar to rehydrate the eggs, if needed.

COOKING TIPS:

- *If you have a slow cooker that holds more than four 1-pint (455-g) jars, or you have smaller jars, you can add more servings. Adjust the recipe as needed.*

- *Use your favorite breakfast meat or vegetables in place of the hash browns and butternut squash for a low-carb breakfast.*

Per serving: Calories: 338 | Fat: 14.6 g | Carbs: 27 g | Fiber: 3.9 g | Protein: 21.2 g

SAVORY BREAKFAST SAUSAGE MEATBALLS

I love having breakfast meatballs on hand for easy, grab-and-go meals. This spice combination is what I use to make homemade Paleo breakfast sausage right at home, too. Simply combine only the spices with 2 pounds (910 g) of ground pork and form into patties to panfry, or keep ground for crumbled breakfast sausage.

SERVES 6

1 lb (455 g) ground pork

1 lb (455 g) lean ground turkey

1 cup (70 g) diced mushrooms

½ cup (50 g) almond flour

½ medium yellow onion, grated directly into the mixing bowl

½ medium apple (Honeycrisp or similar variety), peeled and grated directly into the mixing bowl

1½ tsp (5 g) fennel seeds

1½ tsp (5 g) salt

2 tsp (10 g) ground black pepper

1 tsp rubbed sage

1 tsp garlic powder

½ tsp ground thyme

½ tsp crushed red pepper flakes, or to taste (optional)

1½ tbsp (23 ml) maple syrup (optional)

Add the pork, turkey, mushrooms, flour, onion, apple, fennel seeds, salt, black pepper, sage, garlic powder, thyme, red pepper flakes (if using) and maple syrup (if using) to a large mixing bowl. Be sure to grate the onion and apple directly into the bowl to retain the juices.

Using your hands, combine the mixture and then roll it into 1- to 1½-inch (2.5- to 3.8-cm) balls. Place the meatballs in the slow cooker; start by covering the bottom first and then add a second layer on top. The meatballs can be touching, but don't pack them in too tightly.

Cook on high for 2 to 3 hours or on low for 3 to 6 hours.

These can be frozen raw or after they've been cooked by placing the meatballs evenly spaced on a baking sheet and then placing in the freezer. You can freeze the entire batch or separate them into portions. Once the meatballs have started to freeze, you can then transfer them to freezer-safe storage containers. Raw meatballs can be frozen for 3 to 4 months and cooked meatballs can be frozen for 2 to 3 months.

To reheat, thaw the frozen meatballs in the refrigerator. Then, arrange them on a sheet pan and cook them in a preheated 350°F (177°C) oven for 10 minutes, or until heated through. You can also microwave the thawed meatballs on high for 3 minutes.

COOKING TIPS:

- Omit the mushrooms for a less savory, sweeter apple sausage.
- Swap the almond flour for coconut flour to make these nut-free.
- Use 2 teaspoons (4 g) of gelatin in place of the almond flour binder and omit the fennel seeds for AIP.

Per serving: Calories: 360 | Fat: 18.8 g | Carbs: 5.5 g | Fiber: 1.9 g | Protein: 34 g

BASIL BREAKFAST BAKE

Using chopped basil with the eggs and veggies, and a savory spice mix with the sausage, gives this recipe a bright and fresh yet familiar breakfast flavor. And this make-ahead Paleo breakfast still packs enough protein to keep you going until lunch. If dairy isn't an issue for you, try it with some feta!

SERVES 6

SAUSAGE

1 lb (455 g) ground pork or chicken

1 tsp salt

1 tsp fennel seeds

1 tsp dried thyme

½ tsp ground black pepper

½ tsp ground sage

½ tsp garlic powder

¼ tsp paprika

¼ tsp onion powder

2 cups (300 g) hash browns or shredded potatoes, thawed if frozen

1 cup (70 g) finely chopped broccoli florets

1 cup (40 g) loosely packed chopped basil, plus more for garnish

EGGS

12 eggs

¼ cup (60 ml) dairy-free milk

1 tsp salt

½ tsp ground black pepper

2 Roma tomatoes, thinly sliced

To make the sausage, in a large skillet over medium heat, add the ground meat and all the sausage seasonings. Mix the salt, fennel seeds, thyme, pepper, sage, garlic powder, paprika and onion powder into the ground meat while breaking it apart with a spoon and cook until browned, about 10 minutes. Remove from the heat and drain the excess grease.

Line the slow cooker with parchment paper or coat the insert with nonstick cooking spray. Add the hash browns to the bottom of the slow cooker, followed by the ground sausage, broccoli and basil.

To make the eggs, in a large bowl, combine the eggs, milk, salt and pepper and beat until scrambled.

Pour the eggs over the sausage and vegetables in the slow cooker, ensuring everything is evenly covered. Layer the tomato slices on top.

Cook on high for 2 to 3 hours or on low for 4 to 6, or until the eggs are set.

To freeze, remove the egg bake from the slow cooker using the parchment paper and allow to completely cool. You can freeze the entire casserole or cut it into serving sizes and freeze as individual servings. Store in the freezer for up to 3 months. Thaw in the refrigerator overnight, or up to 24 hours. Reheat in the microwave or oven.

COOKING TIPS:

- *Omit the hash browns to make this low carb.*
- *Use a 12-ounce (340-g) package of bacon, cooked and chopped, in place of the ground meat.*

Per serving: Calories: 346 | Fat: 21 g | Carbs: 8.2 g | Fiber: 2.1 g | Protein: 27.7 g

CHAPTER 2

Paleo-fied POULTRY

This chapter includes some Paleo-fied versions of your favorite familiar chicken dishes, as well as exciting new recipes you haven't seen before. These use both white and dark meat chicken, but almost all chicken slow cooker recipes, with the exception of whole chickens of course, can use thighs or breasts interchangeably by simply increasing or decreasing the liquid and cooking time. Dark meat is almost always going to be more flavorful when it's cooked in the slow cooker than white meat is. While they're both good sources of protein, dark meat has more monounsaturated fat—the "good" kind of fat. This means that white meat dries out faster, so you'll find that the recipes that use chicken breasts also typically call for ample healthy fats or quite a bit of liquid to help prevent this. Dark meat, like chicken thighs, can tolerate lengthy cook times and land on your dinner plate hours later still juicy and bursting with flavor. Just give Charlie's Chicken (page 56) a try and you'll see what I mean. Chicken thighs are next to impossible to overcook, and the worst that happens if you do is that the tender meat simply falls off the bone.

The good news is that this meat that cooks beautifully in the slow cooker is also much more affordable! On average, bone-in chicken thighs, when compared to boneless skinless chicken breasts, cost about one-third of the price per pound (455 g), and boneless thighs are half the cost of breasts. Opting for thighs once in a while will add some flavor to your life and is an economical way to lower the grocery bill without sacrificing anything on the health front. Even better? You can save those bones for homemade broth (page 183).

Some of my favorites in this chapter include Simmerin' Hawaiian Fajitas (page 38), Tandoori Drumsticks with Vinegar Cucumber Salad (page 46) and Chicken Taco Casserole with Homemade Taco Sauce (page 63).

SIMMERIN' HAWAIIAN FAJITAS

We often batch cook a protein on the weekend for simple meals to throw together quickly throughout the week, and this is one of our favorites. Using chicken thighs results in incredibly juicy and tender shredded chicken that falls apart when cooked low and slow with the pineapple. Serve over salads, in collard or lettuce wraps, with a creamy coleslaw, in tacos with grain-free tortillas or in cauliflower rice bowls.

FREEZER FRIENDLY · NUT-FREE · EGG-FREE · SUGAR-FREE OPTION

SERVES 6

⅓ cup (80 ml) pineapple juice

Juice of ½ lime

2 tbsp (24 g) coconut sugar

1 tbsp (15 ml) coconut aminos

1 tbsp (9 g) cumin

1 tbsp (10 g) minced garlic

1½ tsp (3 g) chili powder

1 tsp paprika

½ tsp ground black pepper

¼ tsp salt

1½ lb (680 g) boneless skinless chicken thighs

4 slices cored pineapple, fresh or canned in 100% juice

1 red bell pepper, cored and thinly sliced

1 medium red onion, halved and thinly sliced

Grain-free tortillas (Siete brand), cauliflower rice or lettuce wraps, for serving (optional)

In a small bowl, combine the pineapple juice, lime juice, coconut sugar, coconut aminos, cumin, garlic, chili powder, paprika, pepper and salt.

Place the chicken thighs in the slow cooker and pour the pineapple juice mixture evenly over the chicken. Lay the pineapple slices over the chicken thighs in a single layer. Cover the slow cooker and cook on low for 6 to 8 hours or on high for 3 to 4 hours.

Thirty minutes prior to eating, remove the pineapple slices and dice into chunks. Use two forks to shred the chicken in the slow cooker. Add the pineapple chunks, sliced pepper and onion to the slow cooker and stir into the shredded chicken. Place the cover back on and cook for 30 minutes, or until the vegetables are tender.

Serve in grain-free tortillas, over cauliflower rice or in lettuce wraps.

To freeze uncooked, combine the pineapple juice, lime juice, coconut sugar, coconut aminos, cumin, garlic, chili powder, paprika, pepper, salt, chicken and pineapple slices in a large freezer-safe bag or container. Store in the freezer for up to 3 months. Defrost overnight in the refrigerator, and then pour into the slow cooker and continue cooking as directed, adding the pepper and onion 30 minutes before the cook time is finished. To freeze cooked, allow to fully cool and then store in a freezer-safe bag or container for up to 2 months.

COOKING TIP:

- *Omit the sugar for sugar-free.*

Per serving: Calories: 232 | Fat: 4.9 g | Carbs: 25.2 g | Fiber: 1.3 g | Protein: 23.4 g

RUBBED GARLIC RANCH WINGS WITH HOMEMADE DAIRY-FREE RANCH

Garlic and ranch are a match made for chicken if there ever was one. These wings are made even more amazing with the addition of mayo in the rub. It helps retain moisture on the inside and keeps the garlic and ranch all but glued to the meat on the outside. I have close to two dozen wing recipes on my website, but these are a top favorite, so I think that means you have to give it a shot. (#trustfall??)

SERVES 6

RANCH SEASONING

2 tbsp (3 g) dried parsley

1 tbsp (2 g) dried dill

1 tbsp (9 g) garlic powder

1 tbsp (2 g) dried onion flakes

2 tsp (1 g) dried chives

2 tsp (5 g) onion powder

2 tsp (12 g) salt

1 tsp ground black pepper

RANCH DRESSING

1½ tbsp (23 g) homemade ranch seasoning

¼ cup (60 ml) canned coconut milk

¼ cup (60 g) mayonnaise (I recommend Primal Kitchen brand)

WINGS

2–3 lb (0.9–1.4 kg) chicken wings

3 tbsp (45 g) homemade ranch seasoning

2 tbsp (30 g) mayonnaise

2 tsp (5 g) garlic powder or 5–6 cloves garlic, minced

1 tsp salt

To make the ranch seasoning, add the parsley, dill, garlic powder, onion flakes, chives, onion powder, salt and pepper in a jar. Shake well to combine. Reserve 3 tablespoons (45 g) for the wings. Mix the remaining 1½ tablespoons (23 g) seasoning with the coconut milk and mayonnaise to make ranch dressing.

To make the wings, pat them dry with paper towels and place in a large bowl. Add the reserved 1½ tablespoons (23 g) of ranch seasoning, mayonnaise, garlic and salt. Use your hands to mix and coat the wings really well with the rub.

Place the wings in the slow cooker, first in an even layer on the bottom and then in a second layer by filling in the gaps between the bottom wings. Cover and cook on low for 3 to 4 hours.

To make the wings crispier, transfer the wings to a baking sheet lined with foil, arranging with space between each wing. Broil for 3 to 4 minutes, or until the desired texture is achieved, keeping an eye on them to prevent them from getting too crispy.

COOKING TIPS:

- *If you're in a hurry or don't want to use the oven, for the last 15 to 30 minutes of cooking, you can vent the slow cooker by turning the lid to open a 2- to 3-inch (5- to 7.5-cm) space. This will allow the excess moisture to escape. While they won't get crispy in the same way a broiler would make them, the skin on the sides of the wings that are exposed will firm up.*

- *If you're craving something spicy, replace 1 tablespoon (15 g) of the mayo with hot sauce and add a bit of cayenne and paprika to the ranch dressing.*

Per serving: Calories: 377 | Fat: 28 g | Carbs: 2.2 g | Fiber: 0.01 g | Protein: 28.1 g

WEEKNIGHT HERO
WHOLE CHICKEN

NUT-FREE   EGG-FREE   LOW-CARB   AIP FRIENDLY OPTION   AIP

SERVES 6

This is my family's favorite way to make a juicy, flavorful rotisserie-style chicken right at home. Cooking it low and slow allows you to get dinner going in ten minutes and come home hours later without wondering what you'll have time to make. I call this the Weeknight Hero because not only is it perfect for busy weeknights, it also saves the day with the leftovers for lunches! Use the leftovers in Italian Harvest Chicken Soup (page 45), repurpose them into Chicken Fajita Breakfast Casserole (page 21) or simply shred the chicken, and mix it with some mayo, halved grapes, diced celery and a touch of lemon juice and salt and you've got yourself chicken salad for the rest of the week!

3–4-lb (1.4–1.8-kg) whole chicken, giblets removed

2 tsp (5 g) smoked paprika

1½ tsp (5 g) salt

1 tsp garlic powder

1 tsp onion powder

1 tsp dried thyme

½ tsp ground black pepper

¼ tsp celery seed

Pat the chicken completely dry, inside and out, with paper towels.

Gather 4 pieces of foil that are roughly 12 to 18 inches (30 to 45 cm) long. Crush each one into a sturdy ball. Stop crushing it once you feel resistance from the foil. It should be about the size of your palm. Then slightly flatten the top and bottom to form it into a hockey puck shape. Do this with all 4 pieces of foil and place them in the slow cooker in the 4 corners. These will prop the chicken up off the bottom and allow for rotisserie-style chicken skin because the fat is able to drip away from the chicken instead of cooking in it.

Mix the paprika, salt, garlic powder, onion powder, thyme, pepper and celery seed in a small dish and then rub it into the skin of the chicken all over, including the inside. Continue rubbing the seasoning over the chicken until it's well coated and all of the seasoning has been used.

Place in the slow cooker resting on top of the foil, cover and cook on low for 7 to 8 hours or on high for 4 hours.

COOKING TIP:

- *For AIP, swap the paprika for your preferred spice, such as dried parsley.*

Per serving: Calories: 238 | Fat: 17 g | Carbs: 0 g | Fiber: 0 g | Protein: 21 g

ITALIAN HARVEST CHICKEN SOUP

This simple soup is quick to prepare, and the red pepper and carrots give the broth a hint of sweetness. It all comes together with the chicken and parsley to create a flavorful meal that's ready when you are. This recipe is great with turkey too, and it's such a tasty Paleo soup, you won't even miss the noodles.

SERVES 6

1½ lb (680 g) uncooked chicken breast (about 4 large breasts, frozen is okay)

2 cups (300 g) diced white onion

3 cups (455 g) chopped carrots

2 cups (300 g) chopped celery

2 cups (300 g) quartered and diced zucchini (about 1 medium zucchini)

1 cup (150 g) diced red bell pepper (about 1 red bell pepper)

1 (28-oz [784-g] can) diced tomatoes with liquid

4 cups (960 ml) chicken broth, homemade (page 183) or store-bought

1 tbsp (10 g) minced garlic

1 tbsp (6 g) Italian seasoning

1½ tsp (1 g) dried parsley

½ tsp salt

½ tsp ground black pepper

Place the chicken breasts in the bottom of the slow cooker. Add the onion, carrots, celery, zucchini, bell pepper, tomatoes, broth, garlic, Italian seasoning, parsley, salt and black pepper on top of the chicken.

Stir to combine the vegetables and liquid, being careful to keep the chicken on the bottom. Cover and cook on low for 6 to 8 hours or on high for 3 to 4 hours.

Thirty minutes before serving, remove the chicken breasts, shred with two forks and mix the chicken back into the slow cooker.

To freeze uncooked, combine the chicken, onion, carrots, celery, zucchini, bell pepper, garlic, Italian seasoning, parsley, salt and pepper in a large freezer-safe bag or container. Store in the freezer for up to 3 months. Defrost overnight in the refrigerator, and then pour into the slow cooker, add the tomatoes and broth and continue cooking as directed. To freeze cooked, allow to fully cool and then separate into individual portions if desired and store in freezer-safe bags or containers for 2 to 3 months.

COOKING TIPS:

- *Add 1 (13.5-ounce [378-ml]) can of coconut milk to transform this into a creamy stew.*

- *Swap out the carrots for veggies like eggplant or baby kale for a lower carb soup.*

Per serving: Calories: 224 | Fat: 3.5 g | Carbs: 23 g | Fiber: 6.6 g | Protein: 26.9 g

TANDOORI DRUMSTICKS WITH VINEGAR CUCUMBER SALAD

If you ask me, turmeric, ginger and garlic are a combination you can't go wrong with. Then when you add the other dynamic spices and the creaminess of the coconut milk, the result is this flavorful, tender chicken. Tandoori chicken is an Indian dish that is traditionally marinated in yogurt and then roasted in a clay oven called a tandoor. We're using coconut milk to keep it dairy-free and Paleo-friendly, but don't worry if you don't like coconut—the hefty Indian spices mask the coconut flavor! Garam masala is a blend of spices unique to Indian cooking that can be found in most grocers.

CHICKEN

½ cup (120 ml) canned full-fat coconut milk

3 tbsp (45 ml) lemon juice (about 1 medium lemon), plus optional 2 tsp (6 g) lemon zest

1 tbsp (9 g) garam masala

1 tbsp (9 g) cumin

1 tbsp (9 g) sweet paprika

1 tbsp (9 g) garlic powder

2 tsp (6 g) coriander

2 tsp (12 g) salt

1 tsp turmeric

½ tsp chili powder

12 chicken drumsticks

To make the chicken, combine the coconut milk, lemon juice and zest (if using), garam masala, cumin, paprika, garlic powder, coriander, salt, turmeric and chili powder in medium bowl and stir until well blended.

Score each drumstick by using a sharp knife and making parallel cuts about ½ inch (1.3 cm) apart to allow the marinade to get into more of the meat. Add the drumsticks to a large zip-top bag or a bowl. Pour in the marinade, seal and toss until the drumsticks are all evenly coated. Or stir the drumsticks in the bowl with the marinade, cover the bowl and refrigerate for at least 2 hours or overnight. The longer, the better!

(continued)

VINEGAR-LIME
CUCUMBER SALAD

2 cucumbers, halved lengthwise,
seeds removed and thinly sliced

½ cup (75 g) finely diced red onion

¼ cup (15 g) chopped mint or cilantro

3 tbsp (45 ml) white wine vinegar

2 tbsp (30 ml) avocado oil

½ tsp salt

Juice of ½ lime

To make the cucumber salad, add the cucumbers, onion, mint, vinegar, oil, salt and lime juice to a medium bowl and stir to combine. Refrigerate for at least 1 hour to marinate.

Pour the chicken drumsticks into the slow cooker with any excess marinade. Cover and cook on high for 3 to 3½ hours or low for 6 to 7 hours. Serve immediately with the salad.

The drumsticks are best frozen raw: after combining the chicken with the marinade, place in a freezer-safe bag and freeze for up to 4 months. To freeze cooked drumsticks, allow to cool completely and freeze for up to 3 months.

COOKING TIPS:

- *Place under the broiler for 3 to 5 minutes for crispier drumstick skins, if desired.*
- *Add ½ to 1 teaspoon of cayenne pepper for more heat.*
- *Make a creamy cucumber salad by mixing in 1 to 2 tablespoons (15 to 30 g) of mayonnaise (I recommend Primal Kitchen brand).*

Per serving: Calories: 408 | Fat: 24 g | Carbs: 2.9 g | Fiber: 1 g | Protein: 44.6 g

DAIRY-FREE "CHEESY" PESTO CHICKEN PASTA

I can't get enough of this "cheesy" pesto sauce. Nutritional yeast is a common Paleo substitution for replicating that cheesy flavor, and this recipe is a fun twist on traditional pesto and a light, refreshing sauce for the squash. How you cut the squash will depend on the size and shape of your slow cooker and the squash you use. Check before cutting if the slow cooker is deep enough to hold the squash cut in half, or wide enough if cut the long way. If you're using an oval 6-quart (5.4-L) cooker or larger, it should fit vertically from stem to bottom.

SERVES 4

CHICKEN

1½ lb (680 g) boneless, skinless chicken tenders, or breasts sliced into cutlets and then cut into 2" (5-cm)-wide strips

½ tsp garlic powder

½ tsp dried parsley

½ tsp dried oregano

Salt and ground black pepper, to taste

8 oz (230 g) asparagus, ends trimmed and chopped into 1" (2.5-cm) pieces

½ red onion, chopped (about 1 cup [150 g])

1 cup (150 g) cherry tomatoes, halved

1 medium spaghetti squash

1 tsp extra virgin olive oil

"CHEESY" PESTO

2 cups (60 g) packed fresh basil, plus more for garnish

¼ cup (40 g) pine nuts, plus more for garnish

2½ tbsp (40 ml) lemon juice

¼ cup (40 g) nutritional yeast (can omit for regular pesto)

3 cloves garlic, peeled

½ tsp salt

3 tbsp (45 ml) extra virgin olive oil

2 tbsp (30 ml) water, plus more as needed

To make the chicken, place it in a large bowl and add the garlic powder, parsley, oregano, salt and pepper. Toss to coat with the seasonings. Place the chicken on the bottom of the slow cooker. Add the asparagus, onion and tomatoes on top.

Cut the spaghetti squash in half to fit your slow cooker and lightly coat the cut sides with the olive oil. Place the squash halves on top of the chicken and vegetables with the cut sides facing up. Cover and cook on low for 6 to 8 hours or on high for 3 to 4 hours.

Meanwhile, to make the pesto, combine the basil, pine nuts, lemon juice, nutritional yeast, garlic, salt, oil and water in a food processor and process until smooth. Add extra water to thin if needed and taste to adjust the salt, garlic, lemon juice or nutritional yeast to your preference.

When the chicken is done, remove the squash from the slow cooker and drain any excess liquid from the chicken and vegetables. Use a fork to separate threads of the squash.

Leave the chicken in strips, or dice or shred if desired. Place the spaghetti squash, chicken and vegetables in a large bowl, add the pesto as desired and mix well. Garnish with a chiffonade of basil (basil leaves sliced into thin ribbons) and pine nuts.

(continued)

DAIRY-FREE "CHEESY" PESTO CHICKEN PASTA (CONT.)

To freeze, cook as directed but leave the spaghetti squash threads separate from the chicken and pesto. Combine the pesto, chicken and vegetables in a freezer-safe gallon (3.6-L) bag or container and the spaghetti squash threads in a separate one. Freeze for up to 4 months.

Thaw both meal components in the refrigerator. Once the spaghetti squash is thawed, transfer to a strainer or a nut milk bag and use your hands to squeeze out all the excess water. Mix together with the chicken and pesto in a casserole dish and reheat in a 350°F (180°C) oven for 30 to 40 minutes, or until warmed through.

COOKING TIPS:

- *Swap any of the vegetables for broccoli florets, zucchini, green bell pepper, artichokes or Kalamata olives.*

- *If you prefer your asparagus to be crisper rather than tender, add it to the slow cooker during the last hour.*

- *Make a double batch of the pesto and store half in the refrigerator for 5 to 7 days or the freezer for 3 to 4 months.*

Per serving: Calories: 425 | Fat: 19.4 g | Carbs: 19.5 g | Fiber: 5.3 g | Protein: 46.5 g

TAKEOUT FAKE-OUT CASHEW CHICKEN

Toss out all of your takeout menus and say goodbye to waiting for those Chinese food cartons to be delivered! This easy recipe is my go-to for a takeout fake-out because it's made with better-for-you ingredients, while still giving all that delicious cashew chicken flavor. Plus, what's not to love about Chinese food that's ready when you are? Chinese five-spice powder is available in most grocery stores in the spice aisle. Serve over cauliflower or broccoli rice, garnished with sliced green onion and sesame seeds for a restaurant-worthy dish.

SERVES 6

2 lb (910 g) boneless, skinless chicken breasts, diced into 1–1½" (2.5–3.8-cm) pieces

3 tbsp (24 g) arrowroot flour, divided

¼ tsp salt

¼ tsp ground black pepper

2 tbsp (30 ml) toasted sesame oil, divided

½ cup (120 ml) coconut aminos

3 tbsp (45 g) ketchup, homemade (page 175) or store-bought (I prefer Primal Kitchen brand)

3 tbsp (45 ml) rice vinegar

1 tbsp (12 g) coconut sugar

2 tbsp (20 g) minced garlic

1 tbsp (6 g) minced ginger

1 tbsp (15 ml) honey

½ tsp Chinese five-spice powder

¼ tsp crushed red pepper flakes

1 cup (150 g) unsalted raw cashews

1 tbsp (15 ml) water

Cauliflower or broccoli rice, for serving

Sliced green onions and sesame seeds, for garnish

Combine the chicken, 2 tablespoons (16 g) of the arrowroot flour, salt and pepper in a large bowl or gallon (3.6-L) bag. Stir or shake to evenly coat. Add 1 tablespoon (15 ml) of the sesame oil to a large skillet over medium heat and brown the chicken for 2 minutes on each side. Place the chicken in the slow cooker.

Combine the remaining 1 tablespoon (15 ml) of sesame oil, coconut aminos, ketchup, vinegar, sugar, garlic, ginger, honey, five-spice powder and red pepper flakes in a small bowl. Stir well and pour over the chicken. Stir to evenly coat the chicken with the sauce. Cover with the lid and cook on low for 3 to 4 hours.

Remove the lid and stir the cashews into the chicken mixture. In a small bowl, dissolve the remaining 1 tablespoon (8 g) of arrowroot flour in the water. Pour into the slow cooker and stir into the sauce. Cook for 20 minutes to soften the cashews and thicken the sauce. Serve over cauliflower or broccoli rice and garnish with the green onions and sesame seeds.

To freeze, allow to fully cool and then store in a freezer-safe bag or container for up to 2 months. To reheat, thaw in the refrigerator, then warm in a skillet over medium heat for 10 minutes or in a slow cooker set to low for 1 hour.

Per serving: Calories: 386 | Fat: 15.2 g | Carbs: 21.1 g | Fiber: 0.8 g | Protein: 39 g

WINTER HARVEST CHICKEN DINNER

NUT-FREE OPTION · EGG-FREE · FREEZER FRIENDLY · AIP FRIENDLY · SUGAR-FREE OPTION

SERVES 4

If you love eating seasonally and are as big of a fall and winter food enthusiast as I am, you're going to enjoy this chicken and vegetable all-in-one meal. Hints of nutmeg, maple and cinnamon make it feel warm and cozy, and the sweetness from the butternut squash and apple are the perfect match to balance the tartness from the cranberries.

¾ cup (180 ml) chicken broth, homemade (page 183) or store-bought

2 tbsp (30 ml) melted ghee, homemade (page 180) or store-bought

1 tbsp (15 ml) maple syrup (omit for sugar-free)

3 tsp (9 g) ground cinnamon, divided

2½ tsp (6 g) garlic powder, divided

Salt and ground black pepper, to taste

½ tsp ground nutmeg

4 cups (600 g) cubed butternut squash (thawed if frozen), divided

1 cup (150 g) fresh or frozen cranberries, divided

½ medium yellow onion, thinly sliced, divided

1 large or 2 small Honeycrisp apples, cored and sliced, divided

1–1½ lb (455–680 g) boneless, skinless chicken breasts (see Cooking Tips)

1 bay leaf

Chopped pecans or sliced almonds, for garnish (optional)

Mix together the broth, ghee, maple syrup, 2 teaspoons (6 g) of the cinnamon, 1½ teaspoons (3 g) of the garlic powder, salt, pepper and nutmeg in a small bowl.

Next, add 3 cups (455 g) of the squash to the bottom of the slow cooker and layer half of the cranberries, half of the onions and half of the apple slices on top.

Place the chicken breasts on top, resting on the layers of vegetables. Sprinkle the remaining 1 teaspoon (3 g) of cinnamon and 1 teaspoon of garlic powder over the chicken breasts and season with additional salt and pepper.

Add the remaining 1 cup (150 g) of squash, cranberries, onions and apple on top of the chicken. Pour the broth and spice mixture over the top and place the bay leaf in the slow cooker. Cover and cook on high for 3 to 4 hours or low for 6 to 7 hours. Remove and discard the bay leaf before serving.

This recipe freezes best prior to cooking by adding all ingredients except the broth to a freezer-safe container or bag for up to 3 months. Thaw in the refrigerator, add the broth and follow the cooking instructions.

COOKING TIPS:

- *If the chicken you use is made up of two or three really thick or large breasts, butterfly them to even out the portion sizes and ensure a consistent cook time.*

- *For the months when cranberries aren't in season, dried cranberries (sweetened with apple juice, not sugar) or frozen cranberries will work beautifully.*

- *Swap butternut squash for cubed sweet potatoes or other seasonal produce, such as delicata squash or pumpkin.*

Per serving: Calories: 288 | Fat: 8.9 g | Carbs: 25 g | Fiber: 5 g | Protein: 27.4 g

CHARLIE'S CHICKEN

Chicken thighs are my cut of choice, and they go wonderfully with this flavor combination. The ingredients give the sauce a hint of sweetness and a bit of a kick, creating a tasty balance. These also happen to be our dog Charlie's favorite, which we learned from the hefty vet bill that came after he snatched five of them off the counter when my back was turned. While I don't recommend this recipe for those with four legs, I do know those that only have two will also scarf these down!

SERVES 6

⅓ cup (80 ml) coconut aminos

⅓ cup (80 ml) hot sauce (I recommend Frank's RedHot)

⅓ cup (60 g) coconut sugar

1 tbsp (9 g) garlic powder

1 tbsp (15 ml) red wine vinegar

1 tbsp (15 ml) sesame oil

1½ tsp (5 g) ground ginger

½ tsp onion powder

½ tsp ground black pepper

2½ lb (1.1 kg) bone-in, skin-on chicken thighs (about 6 thighs)

1 tbsp (8 g) arrowroot flour (optional, for thicker sauce)

1 tbsp (15 ml) water (optional, for thicker sauce)

Sesame seeds, for garnish (optional)

Chopped cilantro, for garnish (optional)

Chopped green onions, for garnish (optional)

In a medium bowl, whisk together the coconut aminos, hot sauce, sugar, garlic powder, vinegar, oil, ginger, onion powder and pepper. Place the chicken in the slow cooker, pour the sauce over the thighs and gently toss to coat them.

Arrange the thighs skin side up in a single layer. Spoon some sauce over the top of each thigh so there's a thin layer over the skin. Cover the slow cooker and cook on low for 4 to 6 hours or on high for 2 to 3 hours.

Thirty minutes prior to finishing, spoon another thin coating of the sauce over the thighs and then turn the slow cooker lid so it's slightly ajar. There should be a 1- to 2-inch (2.5- to 5-cm) opening to allow excess moisture to escape.

For a thicker sauce, in a small cup, mix the arrowroot flour and water until the flour is dissolved, stir into the slow cooker, cover and let the sauce thicken for 10 to 15 minutes. Spoon the sauce over the thighs before serving.

If desired, garnish with the sesame seeds, cilantro and/or green onions before serving.

These are best frozen prior to cooking with all the ingredients combined in a freezer-safe container or bag. Thaw in the fridge to marinate the chicken as it thaws, then place in the slow cooker and follow the cooking instructions.

COOKING TIP:

- *For crispier thighs, preheat your oven to broil. Place the chicken thighs onto a lined baking sheet skin side up, with space between each thigh, and baste with the sauce from the slow cooker. Broil for 3 to 5 minutes, until the skin is slightly caramelized. Serve with additional sauce if desired.*

Per serving: Calories: 319 | Fat: 17 g | Carbs: 15.8 g | Fiber: 0.2 g | Protein: 25.3 g

CREAMY TURKEY SOUP

Making soups is by far one of my favorite uses for the slow cooker. Not only are they some of the easiest "dump-and-go" recipes to throw together, they also become so flavorful after the vegetables and meat have hours to let the flavors meld together in the broth. This soup is so good that no one will even notice it's healthy as well! This is also a simple way to use up leftover turkey (or chicken). If you're using precooked meat, simply add it in when you add the kale.

SERVES 6

1½–2-lb (680–910-g) turkey breast or tenderloin

4 large carrots, peeled and sliced (2 cups [300 g])

1 yellow onion, chopped (1½ cups [225 g])

4 celery ribs, chopped (1½ cups [225 g])

2 tbsp (20 g) minced garlic

4 cups (960 ml) chicken broth, homemade (page 183) or store-bought

1 tbsp (3 g) chopped fresh thyme or 1 tsp dried thyme

2 tsp (1 g) dried parsley

1½ tsp (5 g) salt

½ tsp ground black pepper

2 bay leaves

1 cup (240 ml) canned full-fat coconut milk

2 tbsp (16 g) arrowroot flour

2 tbsp (30 ml) water

2 cups (140 g) dinosaur kale, stems removed and chopped (about 6 leaves)

Place the turkey on the bottom of the slow cooker and then add the carrots, onion, celery, garlic, broth, thyme, parsley, salt, pepper, bay leaves and coconut milk. Cook for 6 to 7 hours on low or 3 to 4 hours on high.

Remove the turkey from the slow cooker, place on a cutting board, shred using two forks and then return the meat to the slow cooker.

Whisk together the arrowroot flour and water in a small dish until dissolved. Pour into the slow cooker, add the kale and stir to combine.

Cover and cook for 30 minutes to wilt the kale and thicken the soup. Add an extra 1 tablespoon (8 g) of arrowroot dissolved in 1 tablespoon (15 ml) of water if a thicker soup is desired. Remove the bay leaves before serving.

COOKING TIPS:

- *I prefer to use dinosaur kale here because it's a less bitter variety, but any type of kale would work. Or swap for baby spinach or simply omit.*

- *Not sold on using coconut milk? Swap for 1½ cups (360 ml) of dairy-free milk and additional arrowroot flour to thicken.*

- *You can use chicken thighs instead of turkey. Add your favorite vegetables instead, such as potatoes, zucchini or bell peppers.*

Per serving: Calories: 289 | Fat: 8.1 g | Carbs: 13.5 g | Fiber: 2.2 g | Protein: 40 g

SPICED WINGS WITH CREAMY CILANTRO SAUCE

It's true! You can make delicious wings in the slow cooker! It makes the meat wonderfully tender, and the spices have time to really make the wings flavorful. The thing I like best about making Paleo wings in the slow cooker is that you can make a large quantity at once, which is perfect for game days, easy appetizers for a get-together or freezing half of the batch for later.

SERVES 4

WINGS

1 cup (240 ml) full-fat coconut milk

2 tsp (8 g) coconut sugar, or preferred sweetener

2 tsp (6 g) curry powder

1 tsp onion powder

1 tsp garlic powder

1 tsp paprika

1 tsp allspice

½ tsp ground ginger

½ tsp ground cinnamon

¼ tsp ground nutmeg

¼ tsp ground black pepper

2 lb (910 g) chicken wings

DIPPING SAUCE

½ cup (75 g) cashews (roasted cashews are okay)

⅓ cup (80 ml) canned coconut milk

⅓ cup (15 g) packed cilantro

Juice and zest of 1 lime

To make the wings, combine the coconut milk, sugar, curry powder, onion powder, garlic powder, paprika, allspice, ginger, cinnamon, nutmeg and pepper in a medium bowl. Place the chicken wings into the slow cooker, pour the coconut milk mixture over them and then stir well to evenly coat the wings.

Cover and cook on low for 3 to 4 hours or on high for 2 hours, or until the wings are fully cooked and the meat is almost falling off the bone.

To make the sauce, add the cashews, coconut milk, cilantro and lime juice and zest to a food processor or blender and process until completely smooth. Adjust as needed by adding more coconut milk if the sauce is too thick or more cilantro if a more herby sauce is preferred. Serve as a dipping sauce for the wings.

To freeze, add the coconut milk and spice mixture to a freezer-safe bag or container along with the raw chicken wings. Shake the bag or stir in the container to evenly coat the wings. Freeze for up to 2 months. Thaw in the refrigerator, stirring the chicken and coconut mixture every few hours as able to prevent the coconut milk from separating, and then follow the slow cooker instructions. Serve with freshly made dipping sauce.

COOKING TIP:

- *To get crispier wings, line a sheet pan with foil and set the oven to broil. Carefully remove the wings from the slow cooker and arrange in rows on the sheet pan. Place under the broiler for 3 to 5 minutes. Watch carefully and remove once the edges of the wings have crisped up.*

For the wings (5 wings per serving): Calories: 412 | Fat: 35 g | Carbs: 4.2 g | Fiber: 1.5 g | Protein: 28.5 g

For the sauce (2 tbsp [30 g] per serving): Calories: 83 | Fat: 6.8 g | Carbs: 3.9 g | Fiber: 0.3 g | Protein: 1.9 g

CHICKEN TACO CASSEROLE WITH HOMEMADE TACO SAUCE

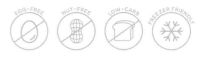

Sauces have this incredibly transformative ability to take a seemingly regular meal and turn it into something crazy-delicious. That's exactly what it does to this spaghetti squash and chicken. With just a few minutes' time and ingredients you can find in your pantry, you'll have a Paleo, additive-free and inexpensive taco sauce. I promise it's going to make your weeknight at least a little bit more exciting.

SERVES 4

TACO SAUCE

1 (8-oz [240-ml]) can tomato sauce

½ cup (120 ml) chicken broth, homemade (page 183) or store-bought

¾ tsp apple cider vinegar

1½ tsp (4 g) chili powder

1 tsp paprika

½ tsp garlic powder

½ tsp cumin

½ tsp salt

½ tsp dried basil

¼ tsp ground black pepper

¼ tsp cayenne pepper

¼ tsp onion powder

¼ tsp chipotle powder, or to taste

CHICKEN

1½ lb (680 g) boneless chicken breasts or thighs

1 red bell pepper, cored and finely diced

½ cup (75 g) diced white onion

1 medium spaghetti squash

Salt and ground black pepper, to taste

1 tbsp (8 g) arrowroot flour (optional, for thicker sauce)

1 tbsp (15 ml) water (optional, for thicker sauce)

To make the taco sauce, combine the tomato sauce, broth, vinegar, chili powder, paprika, garlic powder, cumin, salt, basil, black pepper, cayenne, onion powder and chipotle powder in a medium bowl and stir until combined.

To make the chicken, place it on the bottom of the slow cooker and then add the bell pepper and onion. Pour the taco sauce over the chicken and vegetables evenly so they're all coated.

Cut the spaghetti squash in half, remove the seeds and lightly season with salt and pepper. Place the two halves, cut side up, in the slow cooker.

Cook on high for 2½ to 3 hours or low for 5 to 6 hours. Remove the spaghetti squash and use two forks to shred the chicken in the slow cooker. Next, remove the spaghetti squash threads from both halves using a fork.

If the sauce needs to be thickened prior to returning the spaghetti squash threads, in a small bowl, dissolve the arrowroot flour in the water and pour into the slow cooker. Stir to thicken, and then add the squash threads. Excess water can depend on the bell pepper and type of chicken breast.

Stir to combine, or serve with the chicken taco mixture over the spaghetti squash. Add optional garnishes over the top.

(continued)

CHICKEN TACO CASSEROLE WITH HOMEMADE TACO SAUCE (CONT.)

Salsa, homemade (page 172) or store-bought

Chopped avocado or guacamole

Chopped black olives

Lime wedges

Chopped cilantro

The taco sauce is a great chicken marinade. You can combine the sauce with raw chicken and freeze for up to 3 months. Defrost in the refrigerator. To freeze cooked, store the chicken and spaghetti squash separately. See Dairy-Free "Cheesy" Pesto Chicken Pasta on page 49 for what to do.

COOKING TIPS:

- *Spice it up by adding a 4-ounce (112-g) can of diced green chiles.*
- *The way you cut your spaghetti squash in half will depend on the size and shape of your slow cooker and the squash used. Check before cutting if the slow cooker is deep enough to hold the squash cut in half, or wide enough if cut the long way. If you're using an oval 6-quart (5.4-L) cooker or larger, it should fit vertically from stem to bottom.*

Per serving: Calories: 256 | Fat: 5.7 g | Carbs: 14 g | Fiber: 3.7 g | Protein: 35.1 g

CHINESE CHICKEN "SLOW-FRY"

This is like a stir-fry, except opposite. This recipe has all of the flavors of an Asian-inspired stir-fry but is totally hands-off, mess-free and ready when you are. You can make it your own by using the vegetables you love the most, or change it up by using sliced flank steak instead. No matter how you customize it, it will be a family-favorite Paleo meal you'll feel good serving again and again! Serve over cauliflower rice, broccoli florets or spaghetti squash.

CHICKEN

1½ lb (680 g) boneless, skinless chicken thighs, cut into 1½" (3.8-cm) pieces

Salt and ground black pepper

SAUCE

⅓ cup (80 ml) coconut aminos

¼ cup (60 ml) unsalted chicken broth, homemade (page 183) or store-bought

2 tbsp (30 ml) honey (omit for sweetener-free)

2 tsp (10 ml) toasted sesame oil

2 tsp (7 g) minced garlic

1 tsp grated ginger

1 tsp fish sauce (I prefer Red Boat brand)

1 tsp apple cider vinegar or rice vinegar

½ tsp crushed red pepper flakes, or to taste

½ tsp ground black pepper

6–8 small dried red chiles, seeded and roughly chopped (optional)

2 tbsp (16 g) arrowroot flour

2 tbsp (30 ml) water

To make the chicken, lightly season it with salt and black pepper and then add it to the slow cooker.

To make the sauce, combine the coconut aminos, broth, honey (if using), oil, garlic, ginger, fish sauce, vinegar, red pepper flakes and black pepper in a medium bowl and stir to blend well. Pour over the chicken. Stir in the red chiles if using.

(continued)

2 small heads baby bok choy, chopped into 2" (5-cm) pieces

1 small zucchini, halved lengthwise and sliced

1 red bell pepper, cored and chopped into 1" (2.5-cm) pieces

Sliced green onions, for garnish (optional)

Sesame seeds, for garnish (optional)

Cover and cook on low for 3 to 4 hours or on high for 2 to 3 hours. Thirty minutes prior to serving, stir together the arrowroot flour and water in a small dish and then stir into the slow cooker. Next, add the bok choy, zucchini and bell pepper and stir into the chicken and sauce.

Cover and cook on high for the remaining 30 minutes, or until the sauce has thickened and the vegetables are fork-tender. Garnish with the green onions and sesame seeds, if using.

COOKING TIPS:

- To make the chicken crispier, prior to adding the arrowroot flour to the slow cooker, transfer the chicken pieces using a slotted spoon to a large skillet heated over medium-high heat. Sauté for 3 to 5 minutes, stirring continuously, until the sides of the chicken pieces crisp up. Keep your eye on it, because this is a fast process! After mixing the arrowroot into the sauce, transfer the chicken back to the slow cooker and continue with the directions.

- Dried red chiles are sometimes also referred to as Szechuan chiles and can be found in the international section of major grocery stores. The seeds are what give them their heat, so be sure remove them for a much more mellow infusion of flavor.

Per serving: Calories: 359 | Fat: 14.4 g | Carbs: 21.2 g | Fiber: 1.9 g | Protein: 35.1 g

Beefed-Up MAINS

CHAPTER 3

Beef is one of my favorite things to cook in the slow cooker—it's a staple in my Paleo lifestyle for both the budget and the nutrition benefits. Like chicken, it provides another way to utilize cuts of meat that are less expensive, such as roasts. The best part is that large cuts of meat that contain a lot of connective tissue actually cook better in the slow cooker than they do in the oven. The low and slow method allows the collagen in the tissue to break down, producing a tender, juicy, fall-apart result instead of drying out the meat and making it tough.

That being said, with beef, there's often the extra step of browning the meat first. It's usually optional, except for with ground beef, when browning is required to drain the excess fat. In larger cuts, you don't *need* to brown the meat first, but the added step will always be worth the few extra minutes. It allows the meat to develop deeper, more complex flavors during the long cook time and makes quite a difference in the finished product.

These beef recipes are some of my favorite Paleo-fied renditions of classics, and I know you'll love my Best Ever Beef Ragu (page 88), Sweet and Sour Meatballs (page 80) and Homemade Salisbury Steak (page 83).

PALEO PIZZA MEATLOAF

Meatloaf didn't become an iconic dish for no reason, and my Paleo-fied pizza version takes a good thing and makes it better. I'm partial to cooking meatloaves in the slow cooker because it's much more forgiving than the oven. If you have a loaf pan that fits into your slow cooker, you can use that. Just set the pan inside the slow cooker—don't worry about adding water—and cook per the instructions.

SERVES 6

1 lb (455 g) ground beef

1 lb (455 g) ground pork

1 green bell pepper, cored, quartered and thinly sliced

1 cup (150 g) finely diced white onion

1 (4-oz [112-g]) can sliced black olives, drained

1 egg, beaten

⅓ cup (35 g) finely ground almond flour

2 tsp (5 g) dried minced garlic

2 tsp (2 g) dried oregano

1 tsp dried basil

1 tsp dried parsley

½ tsp crushed red pepper flakes

½ tsp salt

¼ tsp ground black pepper

⅔ cup (160 ml) pizza sauce, homemade (page 178) or store-bought (I prefer sugar-free Rao's brand), divided, plus more for serving and dipping

Coat the slow cooker insert with nonstick cooking spray, or line with parchment paper for an easy way to lift out the cooked meatloaf.

In a large bowl, using your hands, mix together the beef, pork, bell pepper, onion, olives, egg, flour, garlic, oregano, basil, parsley, red pepper flakes, salt, black pepper and ⅓ cup (80 ml) of the pizza sauce. Avoid overmixing the meat, as it dries it out and negatively affects taste and texture. Form into a loaf and place it into the slow cooker. Using a spoon or spatula, cover the top and sides of the meatloaf with the remaining ⅓ cup (80 ml) of pizza sauce.

Cook on low for 6 to 8 hours or on high for 3 to 4 hours. Remove the meatloaf, cover the top and sides of it with additional pizza sauce, if desired, and let cool for 5 minutes before slicing. Serve with more sauce for dipping.

This can be frozen cooked or raw. To freeze raw, assemble the meatloaf up until the step to cover with sauce. Store in a freezer-safe container for up to 4 months. Defrost in the refrigerator and follow the remainder of the cooking instructions. To freeze cooked, allow the meatloaf to fully cool, then store in a freezer-safe container for up to 2 months. To reheat, thaw in the refrigerator and then heat in the oven at 350°F (177°C) for 10 minutes or until warmed through. Or reheat the thawed meatloaf in the microwave one slice at a time on high heat for 2 to 3 minutes.

COOKING TIPS:

- *If the meat mixture is too wet to easily form into a loaf, add another ¼ cup (30 g) of almond flour.*

- *Top half of the meatloaf with sliced pepperoni for non-Paleo eaters.*

- *To make this egg-free, use 2 teaspoons (5 g) of gelatin bloomed in 2 tablespoons (30 ml) of water.*

Per serving: Calories: 357 | Fat: 20.2 g | Carbs: 9.3 g | Fiber: 2.2 g | Protein: 32.5 g

SLOW ANCHO SHREDDED BEEF

The ancho chile, a dried mild poblano pepper, is one of the sweetest of the chile family, and it lends a smoky-sweet flavor to shredded beef in all the best ways. Dried ancho chiles can be hard to find in stores sometimes, so the ground powder is my go-to. If you have whole dried ancho chiles, just use one chile for 1 tablespoon (8 g) of the powder. Serve this over greens, tacos or taco salad bowls, plantain chip nachos or add to a breakfast skillet.

SERVES 6

1 large white onion, roughly chopped

2 tbsp (24 g) coconut sugar

1 tbsp (8 g) ancho chile powder

1½ tsp (5 g) salt

1 tsp cumin

1 tsp ground black pepper

1 tsp Mexican oregano

1½–2 lb (680–910 g) flank steak

1 cup (240 ml) beef broth, homemade (page 183) or store-bought

2 tbsp (32 g) tomato paste

1 tbsp (15 ml) balsamic vinegar

1 tbsp (10 g) minced garlic

Layer the chopped onion on the bottom of the slow cooker.

Combine the coconut sugar, ancho chile powder, salt, cumin, pepper and Mexican oregano in a small dish and mix well. Generously coat the flank steak on both sides, rubbing the spices into the beef with your hands.

Place the coated beef on top of the onions. Add the broth, tomato paste, balsamic vinegar and garlic, carefully pouring in the broth around the beef so as not to wash off the spices.

Cover and cook on low for 6 to 8 hours or on high for 3 to 4 hours, or until the beef shreds easily. Do not stir much while cooking, because the top of the flank steak that isn't submerged in broth will develop a delicious caramelized coating.

Remove the beef from the slow cooker and shred with two forks. Mix the shredded beef with the sauce to coat.

To freeze, allow to fully cool and then store in a freezer-safe bag or container for 2 to 3 months. To reheat, thaw in the refrigerator, then warm in a skillet over medium heat for 5 to 8 minutes or in the microwave on high heat for 3 to 4 minutes, or until heated through.

Per serving: Calories: 284 | Fat: 12.1 g | Carbs: 9.4 g | Fiber: 0.9 g | Protein: 33 g

BETTER-FOR-YOU BEEF BOURGUIGNON

FREEZER FRIENDLY · EGG-FREE · NUT-FREE · LOW-CARB · AIP FRIENDLY OPTION — AIP

SERVES 6

While of course any bourguignon would be much better if you were enjoying it in France, I took what I learned while I was there, tasting as many variations of *boeuf bourguignon* as I could get my hands on, and made a Paleo-fied, alcohol-free version to love right at home. It's every bit as hearty, quick to prepare and will still warm you from the inside out when a comforting meal is in order. Serve over cauliflower mash, mashed potatoes or just on its own.

2 tbsp (30 ml) ghee, homemade (page 180) or store-bought

2–2½ lb (910–1135 g) stew meat or cubed beef chuck

1 tsp salt

1 tsp ground black pepper

2 cups (480 ml) beef broth, homemade (page 183) or store-bought, divided

1 large white onion, diced (about 1½ cups [225 g])

3 carrots, peeled and sliced (about 1½ cups [225 g])

8 oz (230 g) sliced white mushrooms

¼ cup (60 ml) white wine vinegar

1 tbsp (10 g) minced garlic

2½ tbsp (40 g) Dijon mustard

1½ tsp (2 g) dried rosemary

1 bay leaf

½ cup (120 ml) pomegranate juice (optional)

Heat the ghee in a large skillet over medium-high heat. While the ghee is heating, pat the beef dry with paper towels and sprinkle with the salt and pepper.

Once the ghee is hot, place the beef in the skillet in a single layer and sear on both sides, 2 to 4 minutes per side. Do this in batches if your pan isn't large enough. Remove the seared beef and place it immediately in the slow cooker to preserve the juices.

Once all the beef is seared, lower the heat under the skillet to medium-low and add 1 cup (240 ml) of the beef broth to deglaze the pan. Scrape the flavorful browned bits of beef off the bottom and then pour the broth into the slow cooker.

Add the remaining 1 cup (240 ml) of broth, diced onion, carrots, mushrooms, vinegar, garlic, mustard, rosemary, bay leaf and pomegranate juice, if using, to the slow cooker.

(continued)

2 tbsp (16 g) arrowroot flour

2 tbsp (30 ml) water

1½ cups (225 g) pearled onions (frozen is fine)

Cover and cook on low for 7 to 8 hours or on high for 5 to 6 hours. Thirty minutes prior to serving, mix the arrowroot flour and water in a small dish until the flour is dissolved. Pour the mixture into the slow cooker and stir into the sauce to thicken it. Then add the pearled onions, stir, cover and cook for the remaining 30 minutes, or until the pearled onions are translucent and the sauce has thickened. Remove the bay leaf before serving.

To freeze raw, combine everything except the ghee, broth, vinegar, juice, arrowroot and water and store in an airtight freezer-safe container or bag for up to 4 months. Thaw in the refrigerator and follow the cooking instructions. To freeze cooked, allow to cool completely. Store in an airtight freezer-safe container or bag for up to 3 months and thaw in the refrigerator. Reheat in the slow cooker on low for 1 to 2 hours, or until heated through. Or reheat in the microwave on high heat for 5 to 6 minutes, stirring halfway through.

COOKING TIPS:

- *Use 100% pomegranate juice, or cranberry juice as a 1:1 red wine replacement in Paleo cooking. The rich taste deepens flavors and the acidity tenderizes meat in a very comparable way to red wine.*

- *Omit the Dijon mustard to make this AIP friendly.*

Per serving: Calories: 378 | Fat: 22.3 g | Carbs: 14.6 g | Fiber: 2.4 g | Protein: 30 g

PULLED PEPPERED BEEF BRISKET WITH ONION GRAVY

FREEZER FRIENDLY • EGG-FREE • NUT-FREE • LOW-CARB

Brisket is a shining example of how some cuts of meat can be transformed from tough and dry to tender and flavorful when cooked low and slow. The seasonings here are simple, the prep work includes just searing the beef and sautéing the onions and the reward eight hours later is coming home to an incredible-smelling house and an even more incredible meal. Sides to serve with the brisket include mashed potatoes or cauliflower, roasted vegetables or sautéed green beans.

SERVES 6

1 (2–3-lb [910–1350-g]) beef brisket

3 tbsp (45 g) Dijon mustard

2 tsp (12 g) salt

1½ tbsp (15 g) coarsely ground black peppercorns

2 tbsp (30 ml) avocado or olive oil, plus more as needed

1 large red onion, halved and thinly sliced

1 large white onion, halved and thinly sliced

1 cup (240 ml) beef broth, homemade (page 183) or store-bought

1 tbsp (10 g) minced garlic

1 tbsp (15 ml) white wine vinegar

1 tbsp (15 ml) coconut aminos

1 tsp mustard powder

Pat the beef brisket completely dry and rub the Dijon mustard over the entire surface, applying pressure to work it into the meat until the Dijon appears to be almost dry because it's been rubbed in so well.

Next, generously season all sides with the salt and coarse black pepper, which will help form a thin crust during the sear. Let the brisket sit at room temperature for 10 minutes.

Heat the oil in a skillet over medium-high heat and allow it to get extremely hot. Then sear the brisket for 3 to 4 minutes on each side, or until a thin crust forms and the brisket can be easily pulled away from the skillet. Place the brisket into the slow cooker with the fat-cap side up.

In the same skillet, sauté the onions in the remaining beef juices and add an extra 1 tablespoon (15 ml) of oil if needed.

While the onions are sautéing, combine the broth, garlic, vinegar, coconut aminos and mustard powder in a small dish.

Once the onions are softened but not completely opaque, about 4 minutes, place them on top of and surrounding the brisket in the slow cooker.

Pour the broth mixture over and around the brisket, cover and cook on low for 6 to 8 hours. Once done, keep the slow cooker on low, remove the brisket and set it on a cutting board.

(continued)

2 tbsp (16 g) arrowroot flour

2 tbsp (30 ml) water

To make the gravy, dissolve the arrowroot flour in the water in a small bowl. Pour the mixture into the slow cooker with the remaining liquid and onions and stir to combine until thickened.

Just prior to serving, shred the brisket with two forks. If you'd like to slice it instead, cut into thin strips against the grain. Top with the gravy and onions.

Cool the brisket in the remaining liquid or gravy and refrigerate any leftover brisket in it as well. The brisket absorbs liquid and fat, which keeps it tender.

Freeze the cooked brisket with the cooking liquid or gravy in a freezer-safe container or bag. Do not freeze without any liquid or the meat will defrost to be extremely dry and tough. If there is no liquid left, use beef broth instead. Store in the freezer for up to 3 months and defrost in the refrigerator. Reheat in the slow cooker on low for 1 hour or until hot.

COOKING TIPS:

- *Don't remove the fat cap before or during the cooking process. This keeps the brisket from drying out, and it is very easy to cut off prior to serving.*

- *Crisp up leftover brisket in a skillet and add to a breakfast hash or an omelet.*

Per serving: Calories: 448 | Fat: 38 g | Carbs: 6.4 g | Fiber: 1 g | Protein: 28.9 g

SWEET AND SOUR MEATBALLS

These meatballs are some of my absolute favorites. What makes this Chinese-inspired sweet and sour recipe even better is that it's in the slow cooker with relatively little hands-on time. It's almost unbelievable how good these meatballs taste when you know it's a much healthier Paleo option that's not laden with gluten and MSG. These meatballs can be prepared the day before and kept in the fridge . . . if they last that long! Serve over cauliflower rice.

SERVES 6

2 lb (910 g) ground beef

2 tbsp (16 g) almond flour

1 tbsp (10 g) minced garlic

¼ tsp salt

¼ tsp ground black pepper

1 cup (150 g) chopped red onion (cut into 1" [2.5-cm] pieces)

1 red bell pepper, cored and chopped into 1" (2.5-cm) pieces

1 cup (240 ml) pineapple juice from canned pineapple in 100% juice

2 tbsp (30 ml) honey (can omit or replace with 2 pureed dates)

¼ cup (60 ml) white wine vinegar

¼ cup (60 ml) ketchup, homemade (page 175) or store-bought (I prefer Primal Kitchen brand)

1 tsp garlic powder

1 cup (150 g) chunked pineapple

1 tbsp (8 g) arrowroot

1 tbsp (15 ml) water

Sesame seeds, for garnish (optional)

Sliced green onions, for garnish (optional)

Using your hands, mix together the ground beef, almond flour, garlic, salt and pepper in a large bowl until combined, being careful not to overmix.

Roll the mixture into 1- to 2-inch (2.5- to 5-cm) meatballs and gently place them into the slow cooker. Cover the entire bottom of the slow cooker with formed meatballs, placing them side by side. Slightly touching is fine, but do not jam them in tightly. Once the bottom of the slow cooker is covered, add another layer of meatballs on top, slightly staggering the top layer by gently placing the meatballs between the ones on the bottom layer. Add the onion and bell pepper to the slow cooker.

Combine the pineapple juice, honey, white wine vinegar, ketchup and garlic powder in a small bowl. Mix well and then pour over the meatballs.

Cover and cook for 4 hours on low or 2 to 2½ hours on high. Thirty minutes before serving, add the pineapple chunks and cover for the remaining cook time.

Once finished, use a slotted spoon to transfer the meatballs, pineapple and vegetables to a serving dish. Turn the slow cooker to high and thicken the sauce by dissolving the arrowroot in the water and pouring it into the slow cooker. Stir and allow a few minutes for the sauce to thicken and then pour it over the meatballs. Garnish with sesame seeds and green onions, if desired.

To freeze, allow to fully cool and then store in a freezer-safe bag or container for up to 2 months. Reheat in the slow cooker on low for 1 hour or in the microwave on high heat for 3 to 5 minutes, or until heated through.

COOKING TIP:

- *Swap the almond flour for coconut flour to make this nut-free.*

Per serving: Calories: 385 | Fat: 15.8 g | Carbs: 25 g | Fiber: 1.3 g | Protein: 32.7 g

HOMEMADE SALISBURY STEAK

Comfort food really is my love language, and these flavorful steaks with thick, hearty gravy are sometimes just good for the soul. This is a much healthier option than what you'd find in a TV dinner or buffet, but it still has the familiar flavors. It's one of those recipes that people can't believe is Paleo. And somehow these steaks get even better reheated as leftovers after they've sat in the gravy awhile. Serve over cauliflower or potato mash, or with a vegetable side.

SERVES 6

GRAVY

8 oz (224 g) mushrooms, sliced or diced, divided

1 medium white onion, sliced, divided

2 cups (480 ml) beef broth, homemade (page 183) or store-bought

2 tbsp (30 ml) coconut aminos

1 tbsp (15 g) tomato paste

2 tsp (5 g) garlic powder

1 tsp Dijon mustard

¼ tsp salt

¼ tsp ground black pepper

STEAK

2 lb (910 g) ground beef

1 egg, beaten

½ cup (50 g) almond flour

3 tbsp (45 ml) coconut aminos

3 tbsp (45 g) Dijon mustard

2 tsp (5 g) onion powder

2 tsp (5 g) garlic powder

1 tsp dried thyme

1 tsp salt

½ tsp ground black pepper

¼ tsp liquid smoke (optional)

2 tbsp (30 ml) avocado oil

To start the gravy, add half of the mushrooms and half of the onion to the slow cooker.

To make the steak, in a large bowl, combine the ground beef, egg, flour, coconut aminos, mustard, onion powder, garlic powder, thyme, salt, pepper and liquid smoke, if using. Form 6 oblong-shaped patties that are about ¾ inch (2 cm) thick.

Heat the oil in a large skillet over medium-high heat. Once it's hot, sear the steaks on both sides in batches, 3 to 4 minutes per side.

Place the steaks in the slow cooker after they've been seared. Arrange the second layer so the steaks aren't directly stacked on top of each other, but overlap diagonally, leaving open space for the gravy to fill. Place the remaining half of the mushrooms and onions on top.

To finish the gravy, combine the broth, coconut aminos, tomato paste, garlic powder, mustard, salt and pepper in a medium bowl and stir well to combine. Pour the gravy mixture over the steaks, cover and cook for 4 to 6 hours on low or 2 to 3 hours on high.

COOKING TIPS:

- *To thicken the gravy, remove the steaks from the slow cooker, combine 1 to 2 tablespoons (8 to 16 g) of arrowroot powder in equal parts (15 to 30 ml) water, depending on how thick you'd like it, and stir the mixture into the gravy.*

- *Your liquid smoke should list only one ingredient: liquid smoke. I prefer Wright's brand.*

Per serving: Calories: 439 | Fat: 24.3 g | Carbs: 12.4 g | Fiber: 2.1 g | Protein: 37.4 g

MONGOLIAN BEEF AND BROCCOLI

NUT-FREE EGG-FREE LOW-CARB AIP FRIENDLY OPTION (AIP)

Making Mongolian beef at home has never been easier or healthier. The simple sauce tastes anything but—it's loaded with rich and familiar flavors that come together using common Paleo ingredients. The vegetables are added toward the end, so they cook to just the right texture of fork-tender with a hint of that crunch you can usually only get from a stir-fry. Serve over cauliflower or broccoli rice.

SERVES 6

1½–2 lb (680–910 g) flank or skirt steak, thinly sliced against the grain

¼ cup (30 g) arrowroot flour

2 tbsp (30 ml) toasted sesame oil

4 green onions, roughly chopped, plus more for garnish

⅔ cup (160 ml) coconut aminos

⅔ cup (160 ml) beef broth, homemade (page 183) or store-bought

2 tbsp (30 ml) rice vinegar

1 tbsp (10 g) minced garlic

2 tsp (5 g) ground ginger

1 tsp crushed red pepper flakes, or to taste

½ cup (60 g) shredded carrot

1 tbsp (15 ml) honey (optional)

1½ tbsp (20 ml) Paleo hoisin sauce (page 144) (optional)

1 green or red bell pepper, cored and sliced

1 head broccoli, cut into florets

Sesame seeds, for garnish (optional)

Coat the sliced steak with the arrowroot flour by tossing it together in a bowl or gallon (3.6-L) bag. In the slow cooker, combine the oil, green onions, coconut aminos, broth, vinegar, garlic, ginger, red pepper flakes, carrot, honey (if using) and hoisin sauce, if using. Stir well.

Add the coated steak and stir to combine. Cover the slow cooker and cook on low for 5 to 6 hours or on high for 2 to 3 hours. Thirty minutes prior to the end of the cook time, stir in the bell pepper and broccoli. Cover and continue cooking until the beef is tender and the vegetables are tender but still slightly crisp. Garnish with sesame seeds and green onion, if desired.

COOKING TIPS:

- *If you'd like to thicken the sauce, dissolve 1 tablespoon (8 g) arrowroot powder in 1 tablespoon (15 ml) water and stir into the sauce at the end.*

- *Add other veggies like baby bok choy, sugar snap peas, mushrooms or zucchini.*

- *To make this AIP friendly, use olive oil instead of sesame oil, omit the red pepper flakes and swap in a different vegetable for the bell pepper, such as sliced mushrooms.*

Per serving: Calories: 357 | Fat: 16.5 g | Carbs: 14.6 g | Fiber: 1.3 g | Protein: 33.1 g

CHERRY CHUCK ROAST

The slow cooker is the perfect vessel for creating tender, flavorful chuck roasts. The slow and low method allows for this thicker cut to break down into a fall-apart, delicious and healthy roast for you and your family. If you prefer a sweeter flavor for your beef, use frozen dark sweet cherries.

SERVES 6

1 (2–3-lb [910–1350-g]) beef chuck roast

Salt

1 tsp ground black pepper, plus more to season the meat

2 tbsp (30 ml) avocado oil

1 (15-oz [420-g]) bag frozen tart cherries or 1 (14.5-oz [430-g]) can tart cherries in water, drained

½ cup (120 ml) beef broth, homemade (page 183) or store-bought

¼ cup (60 ml) red wine vinegar

2 tsp (7 g) minced garlic

1 tsp dried rosemary or 2 small fresh sprigs

1 tsp dried thyme or 2 fresh sprigs

½ tsp arrowroot flour

1 tbsp (15 ml) water

Chopped fresh parsley, for garnish (optional)

Season the roast on all sides with salt and pepper. Heat the avocado oil in a large skillet over medium-high heat. Sear the roast for 3 minutes on each side and then place it in the slow cooker.

Add the cherries on top of and surrounding the roast.

Combine the broth, vinegar, garlic, rosemary, thyme and 1 teaspoon pepper in a small bowl and pour over the roast and cherries. Cover and cook on low for 7 to 8 hours or on high for 3 to 4 hours. Remove the roast and shred with two forks.

Remove the cherries with a slotted spoon and discard. Pour the remaining liquid from the slow cooker into a saucepan and bring to a simmer over medium heat. Simmer for about 5 minutes, or until the liquid has reduced some.

Combine the arrowroot flour and water in a small dish and stir until the flour dissolves. Pour the mixture into the saucepan. Stir the gravy and remove it from the heat once it has thickened. Pour it over the shredded beef and garnish with parsley, if desired.

If you'd like a thicker gravy, add an extra ½ teaspoon of arrowroot and 1 tablespoon (15 ml) of water and cook until it reaches your desired thickness.

To freeze, allow to fully cool and then store in a freezer-safe bag or container for 2 to 3 months. To reheat, thaw in the refrigerator, then warm in the slow cooker on low for 1 hour, or until heated through.

Per serving: Calories: 409 | Fat: 36 g | Carbs: 9.3 g | Fiber: 1.3 g | Protein: 34.7 g

BEST EVER BEEF RAGU

With a few minutes of preparation and everyday ingredients, you can come home to a rich and incredibly flavorful ragu that you'll want to make over and over again. I'm a comfort food kind of gal, so I don't choose favorites lightly, but I have to say this is easily near the top of the list. It really is *that good*. The best Paleo substitution for the red wine that's used in classic Italian cooking is 100% pomegranate juice, followed by cranberry juice if that's more accessible. Serve over vegetable noodles, Paleo gnocchi, roasted or mashed potatoes or mashed cauliflower.

FREEZER FRIENDLY · NUT-FREE · EGG-FREE · LOW-CARB

SERVES 6

3 lb (1.4 kg) chuck roast, roughly cut into large chunks

½ cup (120 ml) dairy-free milk

½ cup (120 ml) pomegranate juice

½ cup (120 ml) beef broth, homemade (page 183) or store-bought

1 cup (70 g) sliced or diced white mushrooms

1 cup (120 g) diced carrot

1 cup (150 g) diced red or white onion

1 cup (120 g) diced celery

1 tbsp (10 g) minced garlic

1 (14.5-oz [430-g]) can diced tomatoes, drained

1 (6-oz [168-g]) can tomato paste

6 oz (168 g) diced prosciutto

2 tsp (12 g) salt

2 tsp (3 g) dried parsley flakes

1 tsp dried rosemary

1 tsp ground black pepper

1 tbsp (8 g) arrowroot flour

1 tbsp (15 ml) water

Chopped fresh parsley, for garnish (optional)

Place the roast in the slow cooker. Add the milk, juice, broth, mushrooms, carrot, onion, celery, garlic, tomatoes, tomato paste, prosciutto, salt, parsley flakes, rosemary and pepper. Mix everything together just enough to distribute the ingredients around.

Cook on low for 6 to 8 hours or on high for 3 to 4 hours. The beef will shred easily with two forks when it's finished.

In a small bowl, combine the arrowroot and water and stir until the arrowroot is dissolved. Pour into the sauce and let cook on low for about 10 minutes to thicken.

To freeze, allow to fully cool and then store in a freezer-safe bag or container for 2 to 3 months. Garnish with parsley before serving, if desired.

COOKING TIPS:

- *You can use 3 to 3½ cups (455 to 525 g) of frozen soffritto, also known by the French version mirepoix, in place of the fresh celery, carrots and onion. While these mixes are widely available in stores, one of my favorite kitchen shortcuts is to make my own to stash in the freezer for soups, sauces, stews and braising meat. The standard ratio of diced vegetables is 2 parts onion to 1 part each of carrot and celery. DIYing it also cuts down on my budget and food waste by giving purpose to the bunch of celery we never seem to completely get through.*

- *Like most beef recipes, you have the option here to sear the roast and cook the prosciutto before dicing and then adding to the slow cooker. This recipe is great both ways, but searing does help deepen the flavor and is often worth the extra effort.*

Per serving: Calories: 514 | Fat: 40.5 g | Carbs: 10.7 g | Fiber: 1.7 g | Protein: 39.3 g

ALBONDIGAS (MEATBALL) SOUP

Albondigas means "meatball" in Spanish, and since the traditional versions typically include rice, I've been on a mission to create a Paleo option. One thing that really hooked me on this soup is the use of fresh mint and parsley in the meatballs. It adds fresh flavor in a unique way, which really sets this dish apart.

FREEZER FRIENDLY · NUT-FREE · EGG-FREE OPTION · LOW-CARB OPTION

SERVES 4

SOUP

3 cups (720 ml) low-sodium or unsalted beef broth, homemade (page 183) or store-bought

2 cups (480 ml) water

2 cups (300 g) quartered baby blonde potatoes or roughly chopped Yukon gold potatoes

1 (14.5-oz [435-g]) can diced tomatoes with liquid

1 cup (150 g) diced white onion

1 cup (120 g) peeled and diced carrot

½ cup (8 g) loosely packed chopped cilantro, plus more for garnish

2 tbsp (32 g) tomato paste

1 tbsp (10 g) minced garlic

Juice from ½ large lemon or 1 small lemon, plus more for serving

MEATBALLS

1 lb (455 g) ground beef

1 egg, beaten

½ cup (75 g) finely diced white onion

⅓ cup (20 g) loosely packed chopped fresh mint leaves, plus more for garnish

⅓ cup (20 g) loosely packed chopped fresh parsley, plus more for garnish

1 tbsp (3 g) dried oregano

1 tsp garlic powder

1 tsp cumin

½ tsp chili powder

¼ tsp salt

⅛ tsp ground black pepper

Diced avocado, for garnish (optional)

To make the soup, combine the broth, water, potatoes, tomatoes, onion, carrot, cilantro, tomato paste, garlic and lemon juice in the slow cooker.

To make the meatballs, in a large bowl, combine the beef, egg, onion, mint, parsley, oregano, garlic powder, cumin, chili powder, salt and pepper, being careful not to overmix. Form the beef into 1-inch (2.5-cm) meatballs and gently drop them into the slow cooker. Once all of the meatballs have been placed, lightly press each down so that only the very top, if any, of the meatball is exposed.

Cook on low for 6 to 8 hours or on high for 3 to 4 hours. Garnish with additional fresh herbs, a squeeze of lemon juice or diced avocado, if desired.

To freeze, cool the soup completely and separate into individual portions if desired. Store in freezer-safe containers or bags for up to 4 months in the freezer. To reheat, thaw in the refrigerator, then warm in the slow cooker on low for 1 hour, or until heated through. Or reheat one serving at a time in the microwave for 3 minutes on high, or until heated through.

COOKING TIPS:

- *To make use of the whole bunch of mint, double the meatballs and freeze a batch. This also makes it even easier to throw this stew together next time!*

- *Substitute 2 cups (200 g) of green beans cut into 1-inch (2.5-cm) pieces for the potatoes for a low-carb option.*

- *Substitute 2 teaspoons (5 g) of gelatin for the egg to make this egg-free.*

Per serving: Calories: 225 | Fat: 8.4 g | Carbs: 26.4 g | Fiber: 4.1 g | Protein: 20.6 g

BEEF BURRITO CHILI

This is the beef chili I grew up with, but without the canned beans to keep it legume-free. With the flavor packed into this recipe, I promise you won't even miss them. Top your bowl with diced avocado, fresh cilantro and coconut sour cream for a chili with all the fixin's.

SERVES 6

2 tbsp (30 ml) avocado oil

1½–2 lb (680–910 g) ground beef, 90% or more lean

2 tsp (5 g) onion powder, divided

2 tsp (12 g) salt, divided

1 tsp cumin plus 2 tbsp (16 g) cumin, divided

1 tsp dried oregano

3 tbsp (48 g) tomato paste

1 green bell pepper, cored and diced

1 red bell pepper, cored and diced

1 medium red onion, diced

1 (4-oz [112-g]) can diced green chiles, drained

1 (28-oz [784-g]) can diced tomatoes with liquid

3 tbsp (24 g) chili powder

2 tsp (5 g) garlic powder

2 tsp (5 g) paprika

1 tsp ground black pepper

3 cups (720 ml) beef broth, homemade (page 183) or store-bought

Diced avocado, for garnish (optional)

Fresh cilantro, for garnish (optional)

Coconut sour cream, for garnish (optional)

Heat the oil in a skillet over medium-high heat. Add the ground beef and begin breaking it up with a wooden spoon. Season with 1 teaspoon of the onion powder, 1 teaspoon of the salt, 1 teaspoon of the cumin and the oregano and work into the beef as it browns. As the beef finishes browning, add the tomato paste and mix well until the paste thins and evenly coats the beef.

Transfer the beef to the slow cooker. Place the bell peppers, onion, chiles and diced tomatoes on top. Add the remaining 1 teaspoon of onion powder, 1 teaspoon of salt, 2 tablespoons (16 g) of cumin, the chili powder, garlic powder, paprika, black pepper and beef broth.

Cover and cook on low for 6 to 8 hours or on high for 3 to 4 hours.

To freeze, allow the chili to cool, then divide into desired portion sizes and store in freezer-safe containers for up to 3 months. To reheat, thaw in the refrigerator, then warm in the slow cooker on low for 1 hour, or until heated through. Or reheat one serving at a time in the microwave for 3 minutes on high, or until heated through.

Per serving: Calories: 395 | Fat: 21.1 g | Carbs: 17 g | Fiber: 5.5 g | Protein: 34.5 g

PINEAPPLE BEEF SHORT RIBS

These short ribs couldn't be easier to prepare! The pineapple slices help tenderize the meat as it's cooked. You can toss it out after, or chop it up to incorporate into the ribs. Sliced pears could also be used to achieve this same delicious outcome. I love serving this with cauliflower or broccoli rice and coleslaw (page 102); using butterhead lettuce to load the ribs up with toppings for tacos or wraps; or pairing it with a tangy cucumber salad (page 46).

FREEZER FRIENDLY · EGG-FREE · NUT-FREE · AIP FRIENDLY OPTION (AIP)

SERVES 6

2 lb (910 g) boneless beef short ribs

1 medium white onion, chopped

2 green onions, chopped

½ cup plus 1 tbsp (135 ml) water, divided

½ cup (120 ml) coconut aminos

¼ cup (50 g) coconut sugar or (60 ml) raw honey

2 tbsp (20 g) minced garlic

1 tbsp (15 ml) red wine vinegar

1 tbsp (15 ml) sesame oil

1 tsp ground black pepper

4 slices pineapple (canned is okay)

1 tbsp (8 g) arrowroot flour

Place the ribs, onion and green onions in a large zip-top bag. Add ½ cup (120 ml) of water, coconut aminos, coconut sugar, garlic, vinegar, oil and pepper to a medium bowl and stir to combine. Pour the mixture over the ribs, seal and shake to coat. Marinate in the refrigerator overnight, or for at least 2 hours.

Empty the meat and marinade into the slow cooker and wedge the pineapple slices between the ribs. Cook on low for 6 to 8 hours or on high for 3 to 4 hours. Ten minutes prior to serving, remove the pineapple and ribs from the slow cooker.

Combine the arrowroot flour and the remaining water in a small dish and stir until the flour is dissolved. Stir the mixture into the liquid in the slow cooker. Once thickened, pour the sauce over the ribs. Shred the meat or leave the ribs whole.

To freeze, allow to fully cool and then store in a freezer-safe bag or container for 2 to 3 months. To reheat, thaw in the refrigerator, then warm in the slow cooker on low for 1 hour, or until heated through. Or reheat one serving at a time in the microwave for 2 minutes on high, or until heated through.

COOKING TIPS:

· *If using bone-in ribs, I recommend using 2½ to 3 pounds (1.2 to 1.4 kg) for the same amount of servings.*

· *Spare ribs are the pork equivalent to beef short ribs and can be used instead. The major difference is that beef short ribs are typically meatier, and pork spare ribs are typically fattier.*

· *To make this AIP friendly, omit the coconut sugar and swap the sesame oil for melted coconut oil.*

Per serving: Calories: 490 | Fat: 24.9 g | Carbs: 20 g | Fiber: 1 g | Protein: 43.9 g

Protein-Packed PORK

CHAPTER 4

The recipes in this chapter contain some of my favorite Paleo-fied meals I grew up on, but made easier and perfected for the slow cooker! Creamy Pork and Bean Soup (page 98) was always one my family would fight over when my nana made it. The Chili Pork Tenderloin with Strawberry Jalapeño Salsa (page 105) is something I'll never forget having all summer long with fresh strawberries. The Classic Honey Pulled Pork with Creamy Kale Coleslaw (page 102) is probably the first recipe I ever really learned how to make, and it's been a go-to for me ever since. If I have my slow cooker going, it's most likely this recipe you'll find in it!

I know these recipes will turn into some of your family's favorites too. Be sure to make the Smoky Chorizo Chicken (page 106), which I personally love over some mashed potatoes when it starts to get chilly outside!

CREAMY PORK AND BEAN SOUP

My family has a well-loved recipe for pork and bean soup. It was always a special thing when my nana made it for us. Although it's a simple recipe, it's one that reminds me of growing up and taking care of each other through a hearty, nourishing meal. My family's recipe uses beans along with green beans, so I've put my own spin on it to make it legume-free but still delicious.

SERVES 6

1 lb (455 g) green beans, trimmed and cut into 2" (5-cm) pieces

1–1½ lb (455–680 g) center-cut pork chops, cut into bite-size cubes

3 cups (720 ml) beef broth, homemade (page 183) or store-bought

2 cups (140 g) sliced cremini or button mushrooms

1 cup (150 g) chopped white onion

1 tbsp (10 g) minced garlic

½ cup (30 g) finely chopped parsley or 2½ tbsp (7 g) dried parsley, plus more for garnish

1 tbsp (15 ml) apple cider vinegar

1 tsp ground black pepper

Pinch of salt, plus more to taste

1 cup (240 ml) almond milk

2 tbsp (16 g) arrowroot flour

6 slices bacon, cooked and chopped

Combine the green beans, pork, broth, mushrooms, onion, garlic, parsley, vinegar, pepper and salt in the slow cooker. Cover and cook on low for 6 to 8 hours or on high for 3 to 4 hours.

Thirty minutes prior to serving, combine the almond milk and arrowroot flour in a small bowl and whisk with a fork to combine. Stir the almond milk mixture into the slow cooker and add the chopped bacon. Continue to cook for 30 minutes.

Add salt to taste and garnish with additional parsley.

To freeze, allow to fully cool and then separate into individual portions if desired and store in freezer-safe bags or containers for 2 to 3 months. To reheat, thaw in the refrigerator, then warm in the slow cooker on low for 1 hour, or until heated through. Or reheat one serving at a time in the microwave for 3 minutes on high, or until heated through.

COOKING TIPS:

- *For a thicker soup, add an extra 1 tablespoon (8 g) of arrowroot flour.*
- *You can also cook the pork chops whole, and then shred or dice prior to serving.*
- *Swap the almond milk for coconut milk for AIP.*
- *Spice it up by adding a 14.5-ounce (406-g) can of fire-roasted tomatoes and 3 tablespoons (45 ml) of hot sauce, such as Frank's.*

Per serving: Calories: 376 | Fat: 17.4 g | Carbs: 13.8 g | Fiber: 3.4 g | Protein: 42 g

SAUSAGE SUPREME PIZZA SOUP

Focusing on eating real food and prioritizing your health might mean less frequent encounters with the pizza delivery guy, but there are other ways to get your pizza fix. This soup takes a sausage supreme pizza, ditches the gluten-y crust and keeps all of the veggies, so you'll still feel great after dinner. And just like a real pizza, the soup allows for plenty of customization—so go crazy and add your favorite toppings.

SERVES 6

SOUP

1 green bell pepper, cored and sliced

1 red bell pepper, cored and sliced

8 oz (230 g) sliced mushrooms

1 (14.5-oz [406-g]) can diced tomatoes with liquid

1 (2.25-oz [70-g]) can sliced black olives, drained

4 cups (3.8 L) beef broth, homemade (page 183) or store-bought

1 cup (240 ml) pizza sauce, homemade (page 179) or store-bought (I prefer sugar-free Rao's brand)

1 tbsp (10 g) minced garlic

1 tsp dried oregano

½ tsp dried basil

¼ tsp crushed red pepper flakes, or to taste

¼ tsp salt

MEATBALLS

2 lb (910 g) ground pork

1 egg, beaten

½ cup (50 g) almond flour

1 tbsp (3 g) dried basil

1 tbsp (3 g) dried oregano

1½ tsp (1 g) dried parsley

1 tsp onion powder

1 tsp garlic powder

½ tsp fennel seeds

¼ tsp salt

To make the soup, combine the bell peppers, mushrooms, tomatoes and olives in the slow cooker. Add the broth, pizza sauce, garlic, oregano, basil, red pepper flakes and salt. Stir to combine.

To make the meatballs, combine the pork, egg, flour, basil, oregano, parsley, onion powder, garlic powder, fennel seeds and salt in a large bowl. Mix just enough to combine but not overmix. Form into 1-inch (2.5-cm) meatballs, dropping them gently into the slow cooker as you roll them. Gently push the meatballs down so they are covered by the liquid if any of them are more than halfway exposed.

Cover and cook on low for 6 to 8 hours or on high for 3 to 4 hours; do not stir or poke at the meatballs as this could cause them to come apart before they're cooked through.

To freeze, allow to fully cool and then separate into individual portions, if desired, and store in freezer-safe bags or containers for 2 to 3 months. To reheat, thaw in the refrigerator, then warm in the slow cooker on low for 1 hour, or until heated through. Or reheat one serving at a time in the microwave for 3 to 4 minutes on high, or until heated through.

Per serving: Calories: 511 | Fat: 33 g | Carbs: 16.2 g | Fiber: 4.7 g | Protein: 33.1 g

CLASSIC HONEY PULLED PORK WITH CREAMY KALE COLESLAW

This is one of my go-to meals, and I can eat it over and over again and never get bored. My favorite way to eat this is to top the pulled pork with a little BBQ sauce (page 176) and then the coleslaw. It might not be the prettiest meal, but I like to mix it together and enjoy each bite with a little bit of the sweetness from the pork, tang from the BBQ sauce and crunch from the coleslaw!

SERVES 6

PULLED PORK

3 lb (1.4 kg) boneless pork shoulder

2 tsp (5 g) onion powder

1 tsp garlic powder

1 tsp dried thyme

Salt and ground black pepper, to taste

3 tbsp (45 ml) honey

½ cup (120 ml) chicken broth, homemade (page 183) or store-bought

½ cup (120 ml) balsamic vinegar

Easy Peasy BBQ Sauce (page 176), for serving (optional)

COLESLAW

1 (14-oz [392-g]) bag coleslaw mix

2 cups (140 g) stemmed and chopped Tuscan kale, loosely packed

½ cup (120 g) mayonnaise (I recommend Primal Kitchen brand)

¼ cup (15 g) chopped fresh parsley

2 tbsp (30 ml) orange juice (can substitute 1 tbsp [15 ml] honey or omit)

1 tbsp (15 ml) apple cider vinegar

1 tsp celery seed

1 tsp salt

1 tsp ground black pepper

To make the pulled pork, place the pork shoulder on a cutting board. Rub the onion powder, garlic powder, thyme, salt and pepper into the pork and then spread the honey over the top in a thin layer. Place it in the slow cooker.

Pour the chicken broth and balsamic vinegar into the slow cooker on the side of the pork so as not to wash away all of the spices and honey. Cook on low for 6 to 8 hours or on high for 3 to 4 hours.

To make the coleslaw, while the pork is cooking, combine the coleslaw mix, kale, mayonnaise, parsley, orange juice, vinegar, celery seed, salt and pepper in a large bowl. Stir together to incorporate. Cover the bowl with plastic wrap and place in the refrigerator to marinate for at least 1 hour prior to serving.

Once the pork is done, shred and serve topped with the BBQ sauce (if using) and coleslaw.

Per serving: Calories: 392 | Fat: 27.1 g | Carbs: 9.2 g | Fiber: 1 g | Protein: 28.7 g

CHILI PORK TENDERLOIN WITH STRAWBERRY JALAPEÑO SALSA

When you grow up in a place that only has a few short months of summer, you learn to enjoy every minute. For my family, that means the fruity flavors of the warmer months make their way into all of our meals regardless of the season. One of my favorite things about summer is fresh strawberries, and here they're paired with a perfectly seasoned tenderloin for a smoky yet sweet family-friendly meal.

SERVES 6

PORK

2 lb (910 g) pork tenderloin

1 tsp chili powder

1 tsp smoked paprika

1 tsp cumin

½ tsp salt

½ tsp onion powder

½ tsp garlic powder

½ tsp Mexican oregano

2 tbsp (30 ml) avocado oil

SALSA

2 cups (300 g) diced strawberries

½ red bell pepper, cored and finely diced

⅓ cup (50 g) finely diced red onion

1 small jalapeño, seeded and finely diced

⅓ cup (20 g) chopped fresh mint or parsley

1 tbsp (15 ml) extra virgin olive oil

Juice of 1 small lime

Pinch of salt

1–2 tsp honey (optional)

To make the pork, pat the tenderloin dry and place it in a large bowl or zip-top bag. Mix the chili powder, paprika, cumin, salt, onion powder, garlic powder, oregano and oil in a small dish until well combined and then add it to the tenderloin. Rub it into the pork and marinate in the refrigerator for at least 1 hour.

Place the tenderloin in the slow cooker and cook on low for 4 to 6 hours or on high for 2 to 3 hours.

To make the salsa, 30 to 60 minutes prior to serving, add the strawberries, bell pepper, onion, jalapeño, mint, oil, lime juice, salt and honey, if using, to a medium bowl. Stir to combine.

Cover the bowl with plastic wrap and marinate in the refrigerator until ready to serve.

Remove the pork from the slow cooker and slice as desired, and then top with the salsa.

COOKING TIPS:

- *Add diced avocado or kiwi to the salsa. Or use mango or pineapple and omit the strawberries altogether.*

- *The seeds are what make a jalapeño hot. To make this salsa spicier, discard only half of the jalapeño seeds.*

- *The pork seasonings and the salsa are also good on fish such as mahi-mahi.*

Per serving: Calories: 268 | Fat: 12.6 g | Carbs: 7.7 g | Fiber: 1.9 g | Protein: 32.9 g

SMOKY CHORIZO CHICKEN

This hearty meal is a simple way to get dinner on the table with very little effort or hands-on time. The simple ingredients come together in the slow cooker and can be served with sides like cauliflower mash, riced veggies, spaghetti squash "noodles" or baked potatoes.

FREEZER FRIENDLY · LOW-CARB · EGG-FREE · NUT-FREE

SERVES 6

1 lb (455 g) boneless, skinless chicken breasts

12 oz (340 g) chorizo, sliced (I prefer Wellshire brand)

1 cup (240 ml) chicken broth, homemade (page 183) or store-bought

1 (14.5-oz [406-g]) can fire-roasted tomatoes

2 green bell peppers, cored and diced

1 medium white onion, diced (about 1 cup [150 g])

½ cup (120 ml) canned tomato sauce

1 tbsp (10 g) minced garlic

1 tsp smoked paprika

¼ tsp salt, plus more to taste

¼ tsp ground black pepper

Juice of 1 lemon

Place the chicken breasts in the slow cooker. Add the chorizo, broth, tomatoes, bell peppers, onion, tomato sauce, garlic, paprika, salt, pepper and lemon juice on top of the chicken, and stir to evenly combine the spices, leaving the chicken on the bottom.

Cover and cook on low for 5 to 6 hours or on high for 3 to 4 hours.

Prior to serving, shred the chicken using two forks. Stir the chicken back into the slow cooker and add salt to taste.

To freeze uncooked, combine everything except the broth in a freezer-safe container and freeze for up to 3 months. To cook, defrost in the refrigerator and then add to the slow cooker along with the broth. Continue with the remaining cooking directions. To freeze cooked, divide into desired portions and freeze in freezer-safe containers for up to 4 months. To reheat, thaw in the refrigerator, then microwave on high for 2 to 3 minutes, or until heated through.

COOKING TIPS:

- *You can easily make this into more of a stew by adding 2 cups (480 ml) of chicken broth during the cooking process, or prior to eating.*

- *Use kielbasa or Andouille sausage instead of chorizo, if you prefer.*

Per serving: Calories: 262 | Fat: 7.3 g | Carbs: 12.7 g | Fiber: 2.7 g | Protein: 35.8 g

APPLE BUTTER
BBQ MEATBALLS

This recipe really couldn't get much easier. The BBQ sauce does a great job at mellowing the sweetness from the apple butter, creating a slightly sweet, thick glaze. These meatballs are great for a weeknight, but they can also double as the perfect party appetizer at the next cocktail party, football game or holiday get-together—just form into smaller meatballs.

SERVES 6

MEATBALLS

1 lb (455 g) ground beef, 90% or more lean

1 lb (455 g) ground pork

½ cup (50 g) almond flour

1 egg, beaten

1 small white onion, grated directly into the mixing bowl

1 tsp salt

1 tsp allspice

1 tsp garlic powder

SAUCE

1 cup (270 g) BBQ sauce, homemade (page 176) or store-bought (I prefer Primal Kitchen)

½ cup (115 g) apple butter, homemade (page 156) or store-bought (I prefer sugar-free Eden Foods brand)

¼ cup (60 ml) beef broth, homemade (page 183) or store-bought

To make the meatballs, in a large bowl, combine the beef, pork, flour, egg, onion, salt, allspice and garlic powder. Mix the ingredients using your hands, being careful not to overmix. Roll into 1-inch (2.5-cm) balls and place the formed meatballs into the slow cooker next to each other without overcrowding.

To make the sauce, in a small bowl, combine the BBQ sauce, apple butter and broth and then spoon over the meatballs so that all of them are covered. Cover and cook on low for 5 to 6 hours or on high for 2 to 3 hours.

Serve over spaghetti squash, zucchini noodles or cauliflower mash.

COOKING TIPS:

- *If meatballs are too wet to form into balls, add an additional ¼ cup (25 g) almond flour*

Per serving: Calories: 439 | Fat: 23.8 g | Carbs: 18.4 g | Fiber: 4.9 g | Protein: 32.3 g

SIMPLE SMOTHERED PORK CHOPS

I learned to make most hearty slow cooker recipes using copious amounts of canned cream of mushroom soup. Once I started eating Paleo and removing dairy from my diet, I realized that wasn't the healthiest option. By using fresh mushrooms, coconut milk and a combination of spices that mask the coconut flavor, you can achieve that same consistency using real-food ingredients. These smothered pork chops are the perfect example. Serve over mashed cauliflower, mashed potatoes or spaghetti squash "noodles."

SERVES 4

¼ cup (60 ml) ghee, homemade (page 180) or store-bought

4 (¾" [2-cm]) bone-in pork chops

8 oz (230 g) sliced mushrooms

½ cup (75 g) finely diced white onion

1 (13.5-oz [378-ml]) can coconut milk

1 tsp onion powder

1 tsp garlic powder

1 tsp poultry seasoning

½ tsp salt

½ tsp ground black pepper

3 tbsp (24 g) arrowroot flour

1 cup (240 ml) chicken broth, homemade (page 183) or store-bought

Melt the ghee in a large skillet over medium-high heat. Once hot, sear the pork chops for 2 minutes on each side, remove and immediately place in the slow cooker. The pork chops will slightly overlap. Layer the mushrooms on top of the pork chops.

Add the diced onion to the skillet and cook for 2 to 3 minutes, or until translucent. Next, add the coconut milk, onion powder, garlic powder, poultry seasoning, salt and pepper.

Whisk the arrowroot flour into the chicken broth until dissolved and then pour into the skillet. Stir to combine and continue stirring until the sauce begins to thicken. Pour the sauce over the pork chops and mushrooms, cover and cook on low for 4 to 6 hours or on high for 2 to 3 hours.

Per serving: Calories: 537 | Fat: 36.3 g | Carbs: 13.7 g | Fiber: 1.3 g | Protein: 35.4 g

TENDERLOIN CACCIATORE

NUT-FREE EGG-FREE FREEZER FRIENDLY

Cacciatore in Italian loosely translates to "in the hunter style," which is fitting for a recipe in a book all about healthy Paleo meals, don't you think? My variation of cacciatore uses pork tenderloin instead of pork chops for a fall-apart, tender result. Chops, if cut too thin, can easily dry out when left in the slow cooker for too long. The instructions include searing the tenderloin before adding it to the slow cooker. This step is optional, but because of the extra flavor it adds to the meal as a whole, I suggest taking the time to do it. Serve over cauliflower rice or spiralized vegetable noodles.

SERVES 6

2 tbsp (30 ml) avocado oil

2 lb (910 g) pork tenderloin

1½ tsp (5 g) salt, divided, plus more if needed

1 tsp ground black pepper, plus more if needed

1 (28-oz [784-g]) can diced tomatoes, drained

1 green bell pepper, cored and sliced

1 red bell pepper, cored and sliced

8 oz (230 g) sliced mushrooms

1 yellow onion, halved and sliced

½ cup (120 ml) chicken broth, homemade (page 183) or store-bought

½ cup (120 ml) 100% pomegranate juice or cranberry juice

2 cloves garlic, minced

1 tsp dried oregano

1 tsp dried basil

½ tsp dried thyme

1 tbsp (8 g) arrowroot flour

1 tbsp (15 ml) water

Heat the oil in a skillet over medium-high heat. Season the tenderloin with 1 teaspoon of the salt and the pepper and sear until browned, about 2 minutes on each side.

Transfer to the slow cooker and add the tomatoes, bell peppers, mushrooms, onion, broth, juice, garlic, oregano, basil, thyme and remaining ½ teaspoon of salt. Cook on low for 6 to 7 hours or on high for 2 to 3 hours, or until the tenderloin is cooked through. Using two forks, roughly shred the tenderloin in the slow cooker, or remove the tenderloin from the slow cooker and slice it.

Stir the flour into the water in a small dish until dissolved, and then pour into the slow cooker. Stir to combine and thicken the sauce. Season the sauce with salt and pepper if needed.

To freeze, allow to fully cool and then separate into individual portions if desired and store in freezer-safe bags or containers for 2 to 3 months. To reheat, thaw in the refrigerator, then warm in the slow cooker on low for 1 hour, or until heated through. Or reheat one serving at a time in the microwave for 2 to 3 minutes on high, or until heated through.

COOKING TIPS:

- *Use 2½ pounds (1.1 kg) of boneless, skinless chicken thighs to change this into chicken cacciatore.*

- *To make this into a less traditional, creamy cacciatore, add a 13.5-ounce (378-ml) can of coconut milk to the sauce and an additional 2 tablespoons (16 g) of arrowroot flour to thicken.*

- *Use 2½ teaspoons (2 g) of dried Italian seasoning in place of the oregano, basil and thyme.*

Per serving: Calories: 304 | Fat: 10.3 g | Carbs: 17.7 g | Fiber: 4.2 g | Protein: 34.9 g

CHAPTER 5

Super Simple SEAFOOD

Contrary to what some people may think, cooking seafood in the slow cooker is not only possible, it's also ideal for a lot of us who don't want to either mess it up or have to babysit it. Seafood has a short cooking time in the slow cooker. However, there's a larger window to "catch" the fish (see what I did there?) at the time when it's perfectly done and there's less likelihood that you will overcook it.

Many of these seafood recipes are interchangeable with other types of fish, and all of them are great ways to mix up your routine, get different types of protein into your diet and ensure you have an exciting alternative to eating chicken!

COCONUT-LIME-POACHED HALIBUT

Once you poach your halibut in coconut milk, you won't ever do it another way again. The healthy fat in the coconut milk is absorbed into the fish, leaving it buttery and rich. Poaching it this way also allows the other flavors to come through, all without any overpowering coconut taste. This cooking method is great with any mild white fish fillet, such as sea bass, cod, snapper or tilapia. The thinner the fillet, the less time it will take, so check after 40 minutes with thinner fillets like tilapia.

SERVES 4

4 halibut fillets, 6–8 oz (170–230 g) each

2 cloves garlic, minced

Zest and juice of 1 lime, plus lime wedges for serving

½" (1.3-cm) piece ginger, peeled and grated, or ½ tsp ground ginger

1 tsp salt

½ tsp ground black pepper

2 (14.5-oz [406-ml]) cans full-fat coconut milk (enough to completely cover the fish)

¼ cup (4 g) packed finely chopped cilantro

Place the fish fillets in the slow cooker, skin side down. Add the garlic, lime zest and juice, ginger, salt and pepper evenly over the fillets.

Pour the coconut milk into a saucepan and bring to a simmer on the stovetop over medium heat, and then pour it into the slow cooker on top of the fish.

Place the lid on the slow cooker and cook on high for 40 to 60 minutes or on low for 1½ to 2 hours, until the halibut flakes easily and is opaque throughout.

Remove the fish from the slow cooker, sprinkle with the chopped cilantro and serve with lime wedges.

COOKING TIPS:

- *Top with chimichurri sauce instead of lime juice and cilantro.*
- *Transfer 1½ cups (360 ml) of the coconut milk to a small saucepan and bring to a slow simmer. Let simmer for 10 to 15 minutes, until reduced and thickened into a sauce, and pour over the fish prior to garnishing and serving.*

Per serving: Calories: 206 | Fat: 7.1 g | Carbs: 3.9 g | Fiber: 1 g | Protein: 33.3 g

BUTTERNUT-BACON BISQUE WITH SHRIMP

SERVES 6

Bisque is a rich, creamy soup traditionally made with lobster, but in this version I like to load it up with shrimp instead. All of the vegetables make it a filling meal, and the squash and carrots create that rich, buttery texture perfect for fall, winter or really . . . any time! To save on prep time, use some thawed frozen butternut squash.

1 medium butternut squash, peeled, seeded and roughly chopped (5–6 cups [700–840 g])

1 small onion, roughly chopped (about 1 cup [150 g])

2 carrots, peeled and roughly chopped (about 1½ cups [225 g])

4 cups (960 ml) unsalted vegetable or chicken broth, homemade (page 183) or store-bought

½ cup (120 ml) canned coconut milk or almond milk (optional, for a creamier soup)

1 tbsp (15 ml) ghee, homemade (page 180) or store-bought

1 tbsp (10 g) minced garlic

1 tsp rubbed sage

¼ tsp ground thyme

Salt and ground black pepper, to taste

1 lb (455 g) shrimp, deveined and tails removed

6 slices sugar-free bacon, cooked and chopped, plus more for garnish

Place the squash, onion, carrots, broth, coconut milk (if using), ghee, garlic, sage, thyme, salt and pepper in the slow cooker and stir to combine. Cover and cook for 3 to 4 hours on high or 6 to 7 hours on low, or until all the vegetables are tender.

Use an immersion blender to blend the soup in the slow cooker until smooth. Or use a slotted spoon to transfer the vegetables to a blender and blend until smooth. Return the puree back to the slow cooker and stir it into the broth.

Add the shrimp to the soup, cover and cook on high for 30 minutes or on low for 1 hour, or until the shrimp are opaque.

Stir in the chopped bacon, add salt and pepper to taste and serve, sprinkled with more bacon.

To freeze, allow to fully cool and then separate into individual portions if desired and store in freezer-safe bags or containers for 2 to 3 months. To reheat, thaw in the refrigerator, then microwave on high for 2 to 3 minutes, or until heated through.

COOKING TIP:

- *Omit the ghee, bacon and shrimp for a vegan option and add an additional 3 cups (420 g) squash.*

Per serving: Calories: 271 | Fat: 7.5 g | Carbs: 20.5 g | Fiber: 4.8 g | Protein: 29 g

SLOW-HERBED SALMON

Cooking salmon fillets in the slow cooker ensures your fish is tender and cooked to perfection every time. If your salmon comes with the skin on, leave it on while cooking. This will help the whole fillet stay together, and then you can peel it off much more easily afterward. Removing it after cooking also helps ensure as much of the salmon flesh stays intact as possible. Serve with Classic Creamy Scalloped Potatoes (page 136), grilled or roasted vegetables or veggie mash.

LOW-CARB · NUT-FREE OPTION · EGG-FREE · AIP FRIENDLY OPTION (AIP)

SERVES 4

1½ lb (680 g) salmon fillet

½ tsp salt

¼ tsp ground black pepper

3 tbsp (45 g) Dijon mustard

¼ cup (16 g) chopped fresh dill

¼ cup (16 g) chopped fresh parsley

3 green onions, finely chopped

½ large lemon

Season the salmon with the salt and pepper. Thinly coat the flesh of the salmon with the Dijon.

Mix together the dill, parsley and green onions in a small bowl, and then sprinkle it over the salmon, gently pressing it into the fish.

Line the slow cooker insert with a piece of parchment paper that's large enough for the corners to reach slightly up the sides and place the salmon fillet on top. Squeeze the lemon over the fillet.

Cover and cook on low for 2 to 3 hours or on high for 1 hour, adjusting the cooking time depending on the thickness of the fillet used.

COOKING TIPS:

· *You can stack up to two layers of salmon fillets on top of each other to cook in the slow cooker. If the salmon fillet is too long for the slow cooker, simply cut it in half and add another layer of parchment paper and the second piece of salmon over the bottom fillet.*

· *Instead of Dijon and herbs, try a simple fish seasoning of 1 teaspoon each of black pepper, garlic powder, onion powder, salt, celery salt, paprika and coriander.*

· *Omit the green onions and add more herbs to make this AIP friendly.*

Per serving: Calories: 242 | Fat: 16 g | Carbs: 1.8 g | Fiber: 0.5 g | Protein: 3 g

CREAMY CAJUN KIELBASA AND SHRIMP

If you're looking for a laid-back meal, one that has all the flavor without all the work, then this recipe is for you. You can customize it by using Andouille sausage instead of kielbasa and serving it a variety of ways, such as over spaghetti squash "noodles" or mixed into cauliflower rice.

SERVES 4

1 (14-oz [392-g]) kielbasa sausage, sliced

1 cup (150 g) chopped white onion

1 red or green bell pepper, cored and diced

½ cup (60 g) diced celery

1 (14.5-oz [406-g]) can diced tomatoes with liquid

½ cup (120 ml) almond milk

1 cup (240 ml) chicken broth, homemade (page 183) or store-bought

1 tsp paprika

1 tsp garlic powder

1 tsp dried oregano

½ tsp cayenne pepper (optional)

½ tsp salt, plus more to taste

¼ tsp ground black pepper, plus more to taste

1 tbsp (8 g) arrowroot flour

1 tbsp (15 ml) water

1 lb (455 g) large shrimp, deveined and tails removed

Chopped fresh parsley, for garnish (optional)

Add the sausage, onion, bell pepper, celery, tomatoes, almond milk, broth, paprika, garlic powder, oregano, cayenne (if using), salt and pepper to the slow cooker and stir to combine. Cover the slow cooker and cook on high for 3 to 4 hours or on low for 6 to 8 hours.

Stir the arrowroot flour into the water in a small bowl until dissolved, and then add the mixture to the slow cooker. Stir in the shrimp and cook on low for 30 minutes, or until the shrimp are pink. Add salt and pepper to taste. Garnish with parsley, if desired.

To freeze, allow to fully cool and then separate into individual portions, if desired and store in freezer-safe bags or containers for 2 to 3 months. To reheat, thaw in the refrigerator, then warm in the slow cooker on low for 1 hour, or until heated through. Or reheat one serving at a time in the microwave for 2 to 3 minutes on high, or until heated through.

COOKING TIPS:

- *Do not add more liquid if the vegetables aren't covered. They will release liquid while they cook.*

- *Add mushrooms or sliced zucchini.*

- *Use coconut milk in place of the almond milk to make this nut-free.*

- *Add a 12-ounce (340-g) bag of riced cauliflower and an additional 2 cups (480 ml) of broth to transform this dish into a jambalaya look-alike.*

Per serving: Calories: 264 | Fat: 7.9 g | Carbs: 11.3 g | Fiber: 1.8 g | Protein: 36.6 g

SMOKY SALMON FAJITA BOWLS

NUT-FREE · LOW-CARB · EGG-FREE

I've said "this is my favorite" so many times already, but really, fajitas are my favorite. They're such an easy weeknight meal that is made even easier when you throw it all in the slow cooker and spend the time you would be cooking on other things you need to get done—even if that something else is just relaxing on the couch . . . you deserve it!

SERVES 4

2 red bell peppers, cored and sliced

1 green bell pepper, cored and sliced

1 red onion, sliced

1 tbsp (8 g) fajita seasoning

1 tsp chili powder

1 tsp cumin

1 tsp allspice

½ tsp salt

¼ tsp coriander

¼ tsp garlic powder

Cayenne pepper, to taste (optional)

Juice of ½ lime

4 salmon fillets, 4–6 oz (112–168 g) each

Cauliflower rice, for serving

Guacamole, for serving (optional)

Salsa, homemade (page 172) or store-bought, for serving (optional)

Line the slow cooker with parchment paper or coat the insert with nonstick cooking spray. In a large bowl, toss the bell peppers and onion with the fajita seasoning and then place them in the bottom of the slow cooker.

In a small bowl, combine the chili powder, cumin, allspice, salt, coriander, garlic powder and cayenne, if using. Squeeze the lime juice over the salmon, then rub the spice mixture into the salmon to season each fillet.

Lay a piece of parchment paper over the vegetables. The parchment should be large enough for the corners to come up the sides of the slow cooker. Place the seasoned salmon in the slow cooker on top of the parchment paper. Cover and cook on low for 2 to 3 hours, or until the salmon is cooked through.

Remove the salmon by lifting the corners of the parchment paper. Assemble the bowls with the salmon, vegetables, riced cauliflower and any desired fajita toppings.

COOKING TIP:

- *Use white fish such as cod, mahi-mahi or tilapia instead. Adjust the cooking time as needed for thinner fillets.*

Per serving: Calories: 288 | Fat: 15.3 g | Carbs: 11.5 g | Fiber: 2.2 g | Protein: 24.3 g

Set-It-And-Forget-It
SIDE DISHES AND VEGGIES

CHAPTER 6

This section is full of hands-off recipes that can cook while you do something else and can be paired with seared chicken or a grilled steak to help dinner come together quickly. The recipes in this chapter are a mix between easy vegetable side dishes and tasty party appetizers, but the one thing they all have in common is that they can be utilized as a component to your meal prep too.

Some of my favorite recipes from this chapter include Chipotle–Sweet Potato Salad with Lime Vinaigrette (page 128) and Chicken Crunch Cabbage Wraps with Hoisin Sauce (page 144). You'll also find recipes here that would make great additions to your holiday meals, like Rosemary-Balsamic Brussels Sprouts (page 135) and New Age German Potatoes (page 132). The best part is, everyone will love these recipes no matter their dietary restrictions!

CHIPOTLE–SWEET POTATO SALAD WITH LIME VINAIGRETTE

Despite the name, this veggie dish is flavorful but not all that spicy, though you can to tailor the spice level to your liking. Served warm or cold, this is a tasty side salad for summer evenings or paired with a hearty protein for a warm winter meal. Try it served with Chicken Taco Casserole with Homemade Taco Sauce (page 63) or Coconut-Lime–Poached Halibut (page 116). The zesty vinaigrette can be—and arguably should be—doubled to use on other salads or as a delicious chicken marinade.

SERVES 6

SWEET POTATO SALAD

1½ lb (680 g) sweet potatoes, peeled and cubed (about 5 cups [650 g])

1 cup (150 g) diced red onion

1 red bell pepper, cored and sliced

1 green bell pepper, cored and diced

½ cup (8 g) roughly chopped cilantro, loosely packed

2 tsp (5 g) chili powder

1 tsp garlic powder

1 tsp paprika

¼ tsp salt, or to taste

¼ tsp chipotle chile powder, or to taste

1 tbsp (15 ml) olive oil, or more to coat

1 cup (70 g) chopped kale

LIME VINAIGRETTE

3 tbsp (45 ml) olive oil

3 tbsp (45 ml) fresh lime juice

1 tbsp (2 g) chopped cilantro

1½ tsp (8 ml) apple cider vinegar

1 tsp coconut sugar (can substitute with ¾ tsp honey, or omit altogether)

½ tsp garlic powder

¼ tsp salt

⅛ tsp coriander

⅛ tsp ground black pepper

To make the potato salad, add the sweet potatoes, onion, bell peppers and cilantro to the slow cooker and give the vegetables a quick stir to combine. Mix the chili powder, garlic powder, paprika, salt and chipotle powder in a small dish.

Drizzle the oil over the vegetables and then sprinkle the spice mixture over them. Stir well until the vegetables are evenly coated and then cover the slow cooker.

Cook on high for 2 hours or on low for 3 to 3½ hours, or until the sweet potatoes are fork-tender but not mushy. Stir in the kale during the last 30 minutes of cooking.

To make the vinaigrette, combine the oil, lime juice, cilantro, vinegar, sugar, garlic powder, salt, coriander and black pepper in a small bowl or jar, or a salad dressing container if you're doubling the ingredients. Shake to combine. You can store the vinaigrette in the refrigerator for up to 7 days.

Remove the vegetables from the slow cooker. Chill for 30 minutes to 1 hour before combining with the lime vinaigrette if you're serving the salad cold or combine immediately if serving warm.

Per serving: Calories: 295 | Fat: 12.6 g | Carbs: 43.5 g | Fiber: 7 g | Protein: 3.8 g

SESAME-GARLIC BROCCOLINI AND MUSHROOMS

My friend Erin, who makes delicious Paleo recipes at thewoodenskillet.com, got me hooked on broccolini a few years ago. It has a more delicate, sweeter flavor compared to broccoli's more fibrous, bitter taste, which is why it's the perfect veggie to complement this Paleo garlic sauce! The sauce pulls the entire dish together, but it's extremely important to massage the spices and oil into each and every nook and cranny of the broccolini heads, so take your time.

1 lb (455 g) broccolini

2 tbsp (30 ml) olive oil

1½ tbsp (23 ml) coconut aminos

2 tsp (10 ml) sesame oil

1 tsp crushed red pepper flakes

1 tsp garlic powder

½ tsp salt

¼ tsp ground black pepper

8 oz (230 g) sliced mushrooms

1½ tsp (5 g) sesame seeds, plus more to garnish

2 cloves garlic, minced or thinly sliced

GARLIC SAUCE

½ cup (120 ml) chicken broth, homemade (page 183) or store-bought

¼ cup (60 ml) coconut aminos

2 tsp (8 g) coconut sugar

1 tsp rice vinegar

1 tsp sesame oil

1 tsp garlic powder

Pinch of ground black pepper

1 tbsp (8 g) arrowroot flour

1 tbsp (15 ml) water

Trim off the bottom 1 inch (2.5 cm) or so from the broccolini stems. Place the broccolini in the slow cooker. Combine the olive oil, coconut aminos, and sesame oil in a small dish. Pour over the broccolini.

Use your hands to massage the oil into the head of each floret extremely well. Add a bit of extra olive oil if needed.

Sprinkle the red pepper flakes, garlic powder, salt and pepper over the broccolini and massage again.

Add the mushrooms, sesame seeds and garlic and toss to combine. Cover and cook on low for 2 to 2½ hours, or until the broccolini is bright green and fork-tender.

To make the garlic sauce, combine the broth, coconut aminos, sugar, vinegar, sesame oil, garlic powder and pepper in a small bowl. Mix the arrowroot and water together in a small dish. Once dissolved, add it to the sauce and stir to combine.

Once the broccolini is fork-tender, add the garlic sauce and toss to combine. Place the cover so it's slightly ajar with about a 1-inch (2.5-cm) opening, turn the slow cooker to high and cook for an additional 15 to 20 minutes to release the excess moisture and thicken the sauce.

COOKING TIP:

- *If desired, before adding the garlic sauce, spread the broccolini on a baking sheet and broil for 2 minutes to make it crisp.*

Per serving: Calories: 117 | Fat: 9.6 g | Carbs: 12.6 g | Fiber: 2.3 g | Protein: 5.5 g

NEW AGE GERMAN POTATOES

Growing up in Minnesota, where 40 percent of us are of German ancestry, meant I rarely attended celebrations or get-togethers without German potatoes being prepared or being kept warm in a slow cooker nearby. So naturally, this mayo-free potato salad is near to my heart and a reminder of places, people and memories I love. However, I didn't so much love the gluten or the copious amounts of processed sugar used. After making tweaks with real-food substitutions, we're left with a healthier, Paleo version that is just as delicious and very simple to make.

SERVES 6

2 tsp (2 g) dried parsley

1 tsp celery seed

1 tsp salt

½ tsp ground black pepper

1½ cups (225 g) finely diced white onion

1 cup (150 g) diced celery

2–2½ lb (910–1130 g) red potatoes, sliced about ¼" (6 mm) thick

2 cups (480 ml) chicken broth, homemade (page 183) or store-bought

1½ tbsp (12 g) arrowroot flour

⅓ cup (80 ml) white vinegar

⅓ cup (70 g) coconut sugar (see Cooking Tip)

1 tbsp (15 g) Dijon mustard

1 (12-oz [340-g]) package bacon, cooked and chopped

Finely chopped fresh chives or parsley, for garnish

Combine the parsley, celery seed, salt and pepper in a medium bowl. Add the onion and celery and stir to evenly coat. Place a quarter of the potatoes in the slow cooker and layer a quarter of the seasoned vegetable mixture on top. Continue layering until all the potatoes and vegetables have been added to the slow cooker.

Pour the broth into the slow cooker. Larger slow cookers may require an additional ½ cup (120 ml) of broth if the potatoes aren't at least just about covered.

Cover the slow cooker and cook on low for 4 to 6 hours or on high for 2 to 3 hours, or until the potatoes are fork-tender but not falling apart.

Transfer the potatoes to a dish with a slotted spoon, keeping the broth in the slow cooker. Loosely cover to keep warm.

In a small bowl, combine the arrowroot flour and vinegar and stir until the arrowroot dissolves. Add the coconut sugar and Dijon to the bowl and stir to combine. Pour into the broth and stir to combine.

Turn the slow cooker to high and cook for 10 to 15 minutes. Add an extra ½ to 1 tablespoon (4 to 8 g) of arrowroot for a thicker sauce.

Gently fold the potatoes back into the slow cooker along with the chopped bacon. Garnish with finely chopped chives or parsley.

COOKING TIP:

- *If you're omitting the coconut sugar, use only 2 tablespoons (30 ml) of the vinegar.*

Per serving: Calories: 229 | Fat: 4.1 g | Carbs: 44.1 g | Fiber: 4.1 g | Protein: 8.4 g

ROSEMARY-BALSAMIC BRUSSELS SPROUTS

There aren't many, if any, balsamic reductions you can find in the store that aren't made with cane sugar or a plethora of unnecessary preservatives. Making your own is easy, healthier and takes only a few minutes. You can double the balsamic reduction and save half to use for salad dressing, toss it with baked chicken wings or drizzle it over grilled pork chops, chicken breasts, fresh fruit or roasted vegetables.

SERVES 8

2 tbsp (30 g) grainy mustard (with mustard seeds)

2 tbsp (30 ml) softened ghee, homemade (page 180) or store-bought

1½ tbsp (3 g) finely chopped fresh rosemary

2 lb (910 g) Brussels sprouts, trimmed and halved

Salt and ground black pepper, to taste

½ cup (120 ml) balsamic vinegar

2 tbsp (30 ml) honey

Combine the mustard, ghee and rosemary in a small bowl. Place the Brussels sprouts in the slow cooker, season with salt and pepper, and then top with the ghee mixture. Toss the Brussels sprouts to evenly coat. Cover and cook on high for 1 to 2 hours or on low for 3 to 4 hours, or until tender.

Prior to serving, heat the balsamic vinegar and honey in a small saucepan over medium heat. Cook for about 8 to 10 minutes, bringing to a slow simmer and stirring frequently. Remove from the heat when the balsamic has reduced by about half. Do not wait until it looks syrupy while simmering because it will thicken as it cools. Pay close attention as it gets closer to the 8- to 10-minute mark. It begins to reduce quickly toward the end and vinegar can burn if it's over-reduced.

Let the vinegar reduction cool to room temperature, then drizzle over or toss with the warm Brussels sprouts.

COOKING TIPS:

· *You can make the balsamic reduction at any point during the cook time, but no later than 30 to 40 minutes prior to serving so it will have time to cool and thicken before tossing with the sprouts. Or you can make it the night before and either keep it out at room temperature or refrigerate. If refrigerated, allow time for it to come to room temperature before you need it, as it will harden a bit when cold.*

· *Add 3 ounces (84 g) of chopped pancetta to the slow cooker with the raw Brussels sprouts or add 3 or 4 slices of cooked and chopped bacon during the last 30 minutes of cooking.*

· *Toss with ½ cup (75 g) of dried cranberries.*

Per serving: Calories: 160 | Fat: 3.8 g | Carbs: 25.9 g | Fiber: 5.5 g | Protein: 3.6 g

CLASSIC CREAMY SCALLOPED POTATOES

EGG-FREE   NUT-FREE   VEGETARIAN   VEGAN OPTION

I love this side dish because it's easy to prep for the week and then serve alongside my Weeknight Hero Whole Chicken (page 42). Of course, it's also a holiday staple made healthier. Any time I can clear some space and use the slow cooker instead, I'm all in. The cooking time will ultimately depend on how thick or thin you slice the potatoes. If they're on the thinner side, they'll be done sooner, so go ahead and turn that slow cooker to "keep warm" as soon as you notice the potatoes are tender.

SERVES 6

2–3 lb (910–1350 g) golden potatoes, thinly sliced

½ cup (35 g) sliced mushrooms

1 tbsp (15 ml) ghee, homemade (page 180) or store-bought

1 tbsp (10 g) minced garlic

½ cup (75 g) diced white onion

1 (13.5-oz [378-ml]) can coconut cream

1½ tsp (2 g) dried rosemary

1½ tsp (2 g) dried thyme

½ tsp salt

½ tsp ground black pepper

¼ tsp nutmeg

2 tbsp (16 g) arrowroot flour

½ cup (120 ml) chicken broth, homemade (page 183) or store-bought

Arrange the sliced potatoes in rows in the slow cooker insert. Place the mushrooms between some of the potatoes and between the rows.

Melt the ghee in a large saucepan over medium heat and add the garlic and onion. Cook until the garlic becomes fragrant, about 2 minutes, then add the coconut cream, rosemary, thyme, salt, pepper and nutmeg and bring to a simmer.

In the meantime, combine the flour and chicken broth in a small bowl and stir until the flour dissolves. Pour the mixture into the saucepan once simmering. Stir to combine and continue stirring until the cream sauce begins to thicken.

Pour the sauce over the potatoes and gently tilt the slow cooker insert side to side to evenly distribute the sauce between the potato slices.

Cover and cook on high for 2 to 3 hours or on low for 4 to 5 hours, or until the potatoes are fork-tender.

COOKING TIPS:

- *To further thicken the cream sauce, turn the slow cooker to low and set the cover over the top diagonally to vent and allow the excess liquid to evaporate, or dissolve 1 tablespoon (8 g) of arrowroot with 1 tablespoon (15 ml) of water and stir into the slow cooker.*

- *Use olive oil and vegetable broth in place of ghee and chicken broth to make this vegan.*

Per serving: Calories: 281 | Fat: 13.8 g | Carbs: 36 g | Fiber: 2.7 g | Protein: 5.1 g

BUFFALO RANCH CHICKEN DIP

If you're a buffalo chicken lover like me, you'll love this creamy Paleo dip. The slow cooker provides a safe home for the dip if you're traveling to a party or potluck, and then it will keep the dip warm for serving while you're there. You don't need a gathering for an excuse to make this, though! Serve warm with sliced veggies, grain-free chips or crackers or as a meal over a baked sweet potato or greens for a buffalo chicken salad.

SERVES 8

2 tsp (5 g) onion powder

1½ tsp (1 g) dried dill

1 tsp garlic powder

1 tsp paprika

1 tsp dried parsley

½ tsp mustard powder

½ tsp salt

½ tsp ground black pepper

¾ cup (180 g) mayonnaise (I prefer Primal Kitchen)

¾ cup (230 ml) canned coconut cream (the thick condensed cream that's separated from the liquid in a chilled can of coconut milk)

½ cup (120 ml) hot sauce (such as Frank's or The New Primal)

2 tbsp (30 ml) lemon juice

1½ lb (680 g) diced or shredded cooked chicken

1 cup (150 g) diced red onion, plus more for garnish

2 green onions, thinly sliced, plus more for garnish

Chopped cilantro, for garnish

Chopped avocado, for garnish

Combine the onion powder, dill, garlic powder, paprika, parsley, mustard powder, salt and pepper in a medium bowl. Add the mayonnaise, coconut cream, hot sauce and lemon juice and stir until smooth.

In a 3- to 4-quart (2.7- to 3.6-L) slow cooker, add the shredded chicken, red onion and green onions. Pour the buffalo ranch sauce over the chicken and then stir to combine. Cover and cook on low for 2 to 3 hours.

If you want the dip to be thicker, in the last 20 minutes of cooking, slightly tilt the lid so it's almost sitting sideways and allows steam to escape. Garnish with red onions, green onions, cilantro and avocado, then serve warm.

COOKING TIP:

- *To cook the chicken in the slow cooker with the dip, place the raw chicken on the bottom of the slow cooker. In a bowl, combine all the remaining ingredients with the exception of the mayonnaise. Pour the mixture over the chicken and cook on low for 6 to 7 hours or on high for 4 to 5 hours, or until the chicken easily falls apart. Shred the chicken in the slow cooker and turn it to low. Mix in the mayonnaise, cover and cook for an additional 30 minutes.*

Per serving: Calories: 261 | Fat: 21.1 g | Carbs: 3.4 g | Fiber: 1.2 g | Protein: 16.1 g

ZESTY CITRUS BROCCOLI SALAD

Broccoli and cauliflower roasted in the oven can get old after a while, but there's nothing boring about *this* way to get in your cruciferous veggies! I used to dread finding time to cook veggies, and then I'd equally dread having to eat those veggies because I hadn't yet learned that food that's quick and easy to make doesn't have to be boring, and food that's delicious doesn't have to be complicated and take two hours. This warm broccoli salad is punchy, cooked to tender perfection and packed with nutrients and antioxidants. It's brightened up by the fresh, flavorful citrus and is sure to get you out of any veggie rut.

SERVES 6

Florets from 2 small heads broccoli

Florets from ½ head cauliflower

2 red bell peppers, cored and sliced

Zest and juice of 1 large lemon, plus more zest for garnish

1 tbsp (15 ml) coconut aminos

1 tbsp (15 ml) avocado oil

1 tbsp (15 ml) honey (optional)

2 tsp (7 g) minced garlic

1 tsp dried basil

1 tsp salt

½ tsp powdered ginger

4 leaves kale, stemmed and roughly chopped (about 2 cups [140 g])

2 carrots, peeled and thinly sliced into long matchsticks or shaved in ribbons using a peeler

½ cup (8 g) chopped cilantro

Arils from ½ large pomegranate

Segments from ¼ grapefruit or 1 tangerine (optional)

Add the broccoli and cauliflower florets and the red peppers to the slow cooker. Combine the lemon zest and juice, coconut aminos, avocado oil, honey (if using), garlic, basil, salt and ginger in a small bowl, and then pour it into the slow cooker. Massage the mixture into the broccoli and cauliflower with your hands.

Cook on low for 3 to 4 hours or on high for 1 to 2 hours, or until the broccoli is bright green and the broccoli and cauliflower are fork-tender.

Mix in the chopped kale, carrots and cilantro and any additional spices to taste. Cover and cook on low for 30 more minutes.

Toss with additional lemon juice, if desired, and top with the pomegranate arils, grapefruit segments (if using) and lemon zest.

COOKING TIPS:

- *Swap the carrots for parsnips or butternut squash to make this a lower carb side dish.*

- *Omit the red peppers to make this AIP friendly.*

Per serving: Calories: 95 | Fat: 2.7 g | Carbs: 14.5 g | Fiber: 5 g | Protein: 2.8 g

LIGHTENED-UP CAULIFLOWER POTATO SALAD

This may look and taste like a classic potato salad, but it's loaded with lower carb cauliflower in place of potatoes. Making this in the slow cooker gets the cauliflower tender but not overcooked, and it lets the flavors really come together so there's little "cauliflower" taste left! Even better, the eggs hard-boil right in the slow cooker to save you a few steps!

SERVES 6

1 medium head cauliflower

1 tbsp (15 ml) red wine vinegar

Juice of ½ lemon

2 tsp (1 g) dried dill or 2 tbsp (4 g) fresh dill

1 tsp garlic powder

1 tsp paprika

1 tsp salt, plus more to taste

¼ tsp ground black pepper, plus more to taste

¼ tsp celery salt

2 eggs (in the shell)

½ cup (75 g) finely chopped red onion

2 green onions, chopped

½ red bell pepper, cored and finely diced

½ cup (75 g) finely diced dill pickles, plus more to taste

⅓ cup (80 ml) mayonnaise (I prefer Primal Kitchen brand)

1 tbsp (15 g) Dijon mustard

2 slices bacon, cooked and chopped (optional)

Separate the head of the cauliflower from the stem, and cut the head into florets, leaving them in large pieces. Place the florets stem side up so that the cauliflower head is on the bottom and the stalk is pointing up. Pour the vinegar and lemon juice over the cauliflower. Combine the dill, garlic powder, paprika, salt, pepper and celery salt in a small bowl and sprinkle evenly over the cauliflower.

On one end of the slow cooker, gently push the cauliflower closer together to make room for the 2 eggs to rest on the bottom of the slow cooker insert, nested between the cauliflower.

Cover and cook on high for 2½ to 3 hours, or until the cauliflower is fork-tender. Remove the eggs and set aside. Pour the contents of the slow cooker into a large bowl. With a knife, slice the larger cauliflower florets into bite-size pieces. Refrigerate while peeling and chopping the hard-boiled eggs.

Stir the red and green onions, bell pepper, pickles, mayonnaise, mustard, eggs and bacon, if using, into the cauliflower salad. Adjust the salt, pepper or dill to taste. Chill for at least 30 minutes, or until ready to serve.

Per serving: Calories: 133 | Fat: 11 g | Carbs: 9 g | Fiber: 3.7 g | Protein: 2.5 g

CHICKEN CRUNCH CABBAGE WRAPS WITH HOISIN SAUCE

I'm forewarning you—don't expect this to last long if you serve it to guests, bring it to a party or leave it with me unattended. After you fall in love with this chicken and its addicting, perfectly salty and sweet sauce, you will never *not* double the recipe again. And let's not get hung up on technicalities here . . . just because "wrap" is in the official name doesn't mean you shouldn't enjoy the crunchy chicken filling over a salad, or cauliflower rice, or reheated in a skillet with broccoli slaw or zucchini noodles for a quick dinner.

SERVES 6

PALEO HOISIN SAUCE

⅓ cup (80 ml) coconut aminos

¼ cup (60 ml) 100% pineapple or orange juice

3 tbsp (45 g) creamy cashew or almond butter

1 tbsp (15 ml) molasses or honey

2 tsp (10 ml) toasted sesame oil

2 tsp (10 ml) balsamic vinegar or rice wine vinegar

¾ tsp Chinese five-spice powder

½ tsp ground ginger

¼ tsp garlic powder

¼ tsp ground black pepper

To make the sauce, in a small saucepan over medium-high heat, combine the coconut aminos, juice, butter, molasses, oil, vinegar, five-spice powder, ginger, garlic powder and black pepper and bring to a boil. Decrease the heat to maintain a slow simmer and cook for 5 to 7 minutes, stirring frequently, until the sauce has thickened and appears darker. Remove from the heat. Let cool, then transfer to an airtight container and refrigerate for 2 to 3 weeks, or freeze for up to 3 months.

(continued)

WRAPS

⅓ cup (80 ml) coconut aminos

⅓ cup (80 ml) Paleo Hoisin Sauce

1½ tbsp (15 g) minced ginger

1 tbsp (15 ml) rice vinegar

1½ tsp (5 g) minced garlic

2 tsp (10 ml) toasted sesame oil

½ tsp salt

½ tsp ground black pepper

1½ lb (680 g) boneless, skinless chicken thighs, chopped into small pieces

1 cup (150 g) finely diced white onion

¼ cup (25 g) finely chopped green onion, plus more for serving

⅓ cup (50 g) chopped lightly salted cashews

1 (8-oz [224-g]) can water chestnuts in water, drained and finely diced

Green cabbage or butterhead lettuce, for serving

To make the wraps, combine the coconut aminos, hoisin sauce, ginger, vinegar, garlic, oil, salt and pepper in a gallon (3.6-L) zip-top bag or a large bowl. Add the chopped chicken, stir to coat, seal the bag or cover the bowl with plastic wrap and marinate in the refrigerator for 1 to 2 hours.

Add the chicken and marinade to the slow cooker and stir in the white and green onions. If you like your cashews softer, stir them in now. For crunchier cashews, add them at the end.

Cook on low for 3 to 5 hours. Thirty minutes prior to serving, stir in the cashews if you didn't add them earlier and the water chestnuts. Cover for the remainder of the cook time.

Serve the chicken mixture wrapped in green cabbage leaves with more hoisin sauce on the side.

Store the cooked chicken in a freezer-safe container for up to 4 months. To reheat, thaw in the refrigerator, then warm in a skillet over medium heat for 5 minutes, or until heated through.

Per serving: Calories: 269 | Fat: 11.6 g | Carbs: 17.3 g | Fiber: 1.8 g | Protein: 24.4 g

---

LEMON PEPPER PROSCIUTTO WRAPS WITH ROASTED RED PEPPER SAUCE

Kids and adults alike love it when food feels fun, and these veggie wraps play double agent by being both fun to eat and good for you at the same time. Making them in the slow cooker frees up the oven, and the slow cooker can be used to serve and keep them warm too. They're perfect for prepping at the beginning of the week to grab as a snack or have with meals. With the slow cooker, you can really make as many as your heart desires at one time.

WRAPS

8 oz (230 g) carrots, peeled and cut into matchsticks

2 parsnips, peeled and cut into matchsticks

12 spears asparagus, trimmed

2 cups (300 g) trimmed green beans

2 tsp (10 ml) olive oil

1 tsp ground black pepper

Juice from 1 large lime

12 slices prosciutto

1–2 tbsp (15–30 ml) broth or water (optional)

To make the wraps, trim the vegetables so they are roughly the same length.

Add the carrots, parsnips, asparagus, green beans, oil, pepper and lime juice to a gallon (3.6-L) zip-top bag or a large bowl. Use your hands to evenly coat and massage the seasonings into the vegetables. Refrigerate for 30 minutes to an hour.

Lay the slices of prosciutto flat on a cutting board and fold them in half vertically to create long, skinny strips. Gather a small bundle of a few of each of the vegetables and tightly wrap with one strip per bundle.

Immediately place the bundles in the slow cooker, allowing a bit of space between each wrap. They can be close, but not crammed together like sardines. For the second and all subsequent layers, stagger the direction of the wraps so they're not evenly stacked on each other.

Continue doing this until all 12 slices have been used and the veggies have been wrapped.

Cook on low for 3 hours, and then slightly turn the lid to create a 1- to 2-inch (2.5- to 5-cm) gap to let excess moisture escape for about 15 minutes. This will help crisp up the vegetable ends and the prosciutto. Keep an eye on them so they don't dry out during this time.

(continued)

ROASTED RED PEPPER SAUCE

1½ cups (270 g) jarred roasted red peppers, drained

½ cup (75 g) roasted cashews, soaked in water for at least 2 hours and drained

2 tbsp (30 ml) olive oil

2 tsp (7 g) minced garlic

2 tsp (5 g) smoked paprika

2 tsp (2 g) dried basil

¼ tsp salt

1–2 tbsp (15–30 ml) broth or water (optional)

To make the sauce, in a food processor or with an immersion blender, combine the roasted peppers, cashews, oil, garlic, paprika, basil and salt until it becomes a smooth but slightly chunky sauce. Add 1 to 2 tablespoons (15 to 30 ml) of broth or water if you'd like it thinner.

Serve the wraps warm with the sauce for dipping.

COOKING TIP:

- *The sauce is delicious on fish, chicken and vegetables. Double the batch for later or freeze for up to 1 month.*

Per serving: Calories: 117 | Fat: 6.2 g | Carbs: 8.2 g | Fiber: 2.9 g | Protein: 9.3 g

Slow-Cooked SWEET TREATS

CHAPTER 6

Surprise, surprise! The slow cooker isn't just for roasts and stews! It can be used to make treats and sweets . . . the kind that won't sabotage your health. The recipes in this chapter are all easy to whip up and throw into the slow cooker, without using up precious oven space during the holidays when you want to make fudge (page 159) or requiring your oven to be on in the summer when you want to make a berry cobbler (page 160).

There's something to love here for everyone, with my absolute favorites being my Double Chocolate Banana Bread (page 164) and Paleo-Perfect Pear Crisp (page 167).

SEASONAL FRUIT PRESERVES

Looking for a way to use all that fruit your garden is producing or the seasonal fruits that are on sale at the store? Slow cooker jam is your answer! There's no simpler way to make jam than this, and there's no shortage of flavor combinations you can create. I love enjoying it with Paleo yogurt (page 22), using it to make a pan sauce or glaze for meat, over Paleo pancakes, mixed with oil and vinegar for a salad dressing, as a marinade for chicken wings and more!

MAKES 2 CUPS (470 G)

1 lb (455 g) fruit (see sidebar)

1 tbsp (8 g) chia seeds

3–4 dates, pitted and chopped, or 2 tsp (14 ml) honey

Add the fruit, chia seeds and dates to the slow cooker and stir well. Cook on low for 3 hours or on high for 1½ hours, or until all of the fruit has completely softened.

Use an immersion blender, or transfer to a food processor or blender, and blend the jam to your desired consistency.

Store in the refrigerator in an airtight container. The jam will thicken in the refrigerator after 8 to 12 hours. It will keep refrigerated for up to 1 month.

Allow the jam to cool completely. Store in freezer-safe bags or containers, leaving ½ inch (1.3 cm) of free space at the top to allow for expansion. Freeze for up to 6 months.

SEASONAL FRUIT JAM IDEAS

Summer: Blueberry, mango, strawberry, raspberry, cherry
Fall: Grape, pear, plum, peach
Winter: Orange, plum, cranberry
Spring: Apricot, rhubarb, strawberry

Get creative and try out a strawberry basil jam by adding 1 cup (30 g) of basil leaves, a chocolate raspberry jam by adding ¼ cup (25 g) of cacao powder or a blueberry lemon jam by adding 2 to 3 tablespoons (30 to 45 ml) of lemon juice.

COOKING TIPS:

- *Refrain from adding water or the jam will be too thin.*

- *You can omit the chia seeds if you prefer, but the jam will be thinner without them. To thicken the seedless jam, simply strain out the liquid prior to blending the fruit.*

Nutrition values vary depending on the fruit used.

FLOURLESS ALMOND BUTTER BROWNIES

Anybody who has tried to bake with Paleo flours knows how difficult it may be. Baking in general is often a much more specific art than cooking, and using alternative flours can add another layer of complexity. With these brownies, we're nixing the flour altogether and using almond butter instead! It makes a gooey, thick and almost fudgelike brownie that will be a hit with your family or at any potluck!

MAKES 10 BROWNIES

1 cup (260 g) almond butter

2 eggs

¼ cup (30 g) cacao powder or unsweetened cocoa powder

½ cup (100 g) coconut sugar

2 tbsp (30 ml) ghee, homemade (page 180) or store-bought

1 tsp vanilla extract

⅓ cup (55 g) dairy-free chocolate chips (optional, I like Enjoy Life brand)

In a large bowl, add the almond butter, eggs, cacao, sugar, ghee, vanilla and chocolate chips, if using, and stir to blend well. The batter will be thick.

Line a 2- to 3-quart (1.8- to 2.7-L) slow cooker with parchment paper and add the batter to the slow cooker, patting it down with your fingers to evenly distribute. Cook on low for 3 to 4 hours, or until the middle has set and slightly hardened.

Remove from the slow cooker using the sides of the parchment paper and let rest in the paper to cool. Cut into wedges. Store in the refrigerator for up to 2 weeks.

To freeze the entire batch before slicing, allow to fully cool and then wrap the entire brownie in the parchment paper and place in a freezer-safe container. To freeze the brownies once they've been sliced, first place them on a baking sheet, ensuring they aren't crowded, and place in the freezer for 15 minutes. Once they're somewhat hardened, place the brownies in a freezer-safe bag or container and freeze for 2 to 3 months.

COOKING TIP:

• *Use coconut oil instead of ghee to make this vegan.*

Per serving: Calories: 250 | Fat: 18 g | Carbs: 15.3 g | Fiber: 4.1 g | Protein: 7.3 g

AUTUMN'S FINEST
APPLE BUTTER

Nothing says fall like apple butter. I've been making it for years with the apples we always pick at the orchard, but it wasn't until I started eating Paleo that I realized I didn't *really* need all the sugar I was used to dumping in with it. I finally learned to enjoy the naturally sweet flavor of apples, and cooking them low and slow in the slow cooker pulls that flavor out even more. You'll notice the apples get dark in color and almost caramelized. Before you blend, take a little taste and enjoy that sweet, free-from-artificial-sugar taste!

MAKES 2 CUPS (470 G)

3 lb (1.4 kg) Gala or Fuji apples, cored and roughly chopped (peeled or unpeeled, as desired)

¼ cup (60 ml) water

1½ tsp (4 g) ground cinnamon

1 tsp ground nutmeg

½ tsp ground ginger

¼ tsp ground cloves

Pinch of salt

Add the apples, water, cinnamon, nutmeg, ginger, cloves and salt to the slow cooker and stir to combine. Cover and cook on low for 3 to 4 hours, or until the apples are extremely tender and very dark in color. Use an immersion blender to blend the apples in the slow cooker until smooth.

Cover the slow cooker, leaving the lid slightly off center to allow it to vent. Cook on low for an additional 2 to 3 hours to allow the excess water to evaporate and the apples to thicken into a soft butter texture.

Store in an airtight container in the refrigerator for 2 weeks, or freeze for up to 3 months.

COOKING TIP:

- *If you don't have an immersion blender, you can transfer the apples to a food processor or blender and then return the mixture to the slow cooker. You can peel the apples if you prefer, but leaving the skin on works just fine as well!*

Per 2-tbsp (30-g) serving: Calories: 48 | Fat: 0 g | Carbs: 12 g | Fiber: 2.3 g | Protein: 0.2 g

TOASTED COCONUT–MOCHA FUDGE

Making fudge in the slow cooker is so much easier than on the stovetop. It doesn't need to be babysat, and the low temperature of the slow cooker guarantees that your fudge won't ever burn or scorch. There are so many fun ways to flavor it and make it your own. You can use this recipe as a template, and swap ingredients in and out as you like. Near the holidays, I like to add peppermint extract and layer peppermint candies on the bottom, or mix in chopped cherries to make a cherry chocolate fudge. Go crazy—the fudge is your oyster (or something like that).

MAKES 16 PIECES

4 cups (670 g) chocolate chips (Enjoy Life brand is dairy-, soy-, nut- and gluten-free)

¾ cup (180 ml) canned full-fat coconut milk, blended well

⅓ cup (80 ml) honey

2 tbsp (6 g) finely ground coffee

¼ tsp salt

1 tsp vanilla extract

1½ cups (120 g) unsweetened shredded coconut (optional)

Line a 2- to 4-quart (1.8- to 3.6-L) slow cooker with parchment paper. Combine the chocolate chips, coconut milk, honey, coffee and salt in a large bowl and stir to blend well. Pour into the slow cooker. Cover and cook on high for 2 hours or on low for 4 hours.

Add the vanilla and whisk until smooth. Continue whisking until the chocolate doesn't appear glossy on top, about 5 minutes.

Turn off the slow cooker, leave it uncovered and let cool.

To toast the optional coconut, spread it in a small saucepan and heat over medium heat, about 3 to 4 minutes. Gently stir the coconut constantly as it begins to toast. Move the saucepan from the burner and continue stirring, as the coconut will continue to toast. Remove it from the pan and sprinkle in an even layer over the chocolate, if desired.

Once cooled, place the slow cooker insert into the fridge to solidify the fudge, 3 to 4 hours. Then you can remove using the parchment paper, flipping the fudge over so the coconut layer is on the bottom, and slice it into desired pieces.

Keep in the refrigerator for up to 2 weeks, or store in the freezer for up to 3 months.

COOKING TIP:

· *Use coconut sugar instead of honey to make it vegan.*

Per serving: Calories: 436 | Fat: 29.2 g | Carbs: 40 g | Fiber: 1.9 g | Protein: 4.9 g

COUNTERTOP
BERRY COBBLER

If there's one Paleo dessert I could eat every day, it's this berry cobbler. It's incredibly easy to toss together and naturally sweet. The honey serves to bind the berries together and creates a thick, can't-get-enough fruity sauce.

SERVES 4

FILLING

1½ cups (185 g) fresh or frozen raspberries

2 cups (300 g) fresh or frozen blueberries

¼ cup (60 ml) honey

½ tsp tapioca flour

TOPPING

¾ cup (75 g) almond flour

½ cup (50 g) tapioca flour

¼ cup (50 g) coconut sugar

1½ tsp (4 g) ground cinnamon

1 tsp baking powder

⅛ tsp salt

⅓ cup (80 ml) ghee, homemade (page 180) or store-bought

1½ tbsp (23 ml) dairy-free milk

1½ tsp (8 ml) vanilla extract

To make the filling, combine the raspberries, blueberries, honey and flour in the slow cooker insert. Turn the slow cooker on high while you make the topping to help warm the honey so it's easier to mix with the fruit.

To make the topping, add the flours, sugar, cinnamon, baking powder and salt to a medium bowl and stir well to combine. Add the ghee, milk and vanilla. Stir into the dry ingredients to combine into a batter, being careful not to overmix.

The honey and berry mixture will be warm by now. Finish stirring the berries and honey together to evenly distribute the honey.

Dollop the batter on top of the berries and gently spread it so the batter is covering the majority of the berries without being spread too thin.

Cover and cook on low for 3 to 4 hours or on high for 1½ to 2 hours, or until the top layer has hardened but is still soft. Serve immediately.

Per serving: Calories: 316 | Fat: 17.9 g | Carbs: 38 g | Fiber: 4.5 g | Protein: 4.8 g

PUMPKIN-MAPLE PUDDING

The classic combination of pumpkin and maple is one I'll never turn down. These pudding cups make the perfect dessert, filling snack or just-because treat. They can even be frozen into a pumpkin-y, creamy ice pop.

1 (15-oz [420-g]) can pure pumpkin puree

1 (13.5-oz [378-ml]) can full-fat coconut milk

2 eggs

¼ cup (60 ml) pure maple syrup

2 tsp (10 ml) vanilla extract

1 tsp ground cinnamon

½ tsp ground ginger

½ tsp ground nutmeg

Line the slow cooker with parchment paper or coat the insert with nonstick cooking spray.

Add the pumpkin puree, coconut milk, eggs, maple syrup, vanilla, cinnamon, ginger and nutmeg to a medium mixing bowl. Stir well to combine until the eggs are beaten into the pudding mixture.

Pour the pudding into the slow cooker and cover. Cook on low for 2½ to 3½ hours, or until the top of the pudding is set but still bounces back when lightly pressed.

Transfer the pudding to a large bowl, or spoon it into 6 individual serving dishes. Refrigerate until completely chilled and the consistency is firm and creamy, 30 minutes to 1 hour.

COOKING TIP:

- Use 2 teaspoons (5 g) of pumpkin pie spice instead of the cinnamon, ginger and nutmeg.

Per serving: Calories: 201 | Fat: 12.7 g | Carbs: 12.5 g | Fiber: 0.6 g | Protein: 3.3 g

DOUBLE CHOCOLATE
BANANA BREAD

Everybody thinks their mom's, their grandma's or their own banana bread is the best, and I won't try to change your mind. Hey, even I think my mom's is the best. So, while I won't try to beat your nana in a banana bread bake-off, I will tell you that this version is definitely worth a shot. It's Justin's favorite, and every time I make it he doesn't stop telling people about it, so that's gotta count for something, right? This variation was born from my own dislike of banana bread that's "too banana-y" and the happy coincidence of walnuts that were sitting on my counter.

SERVES 8

3 ripe bananas (slightly browning works best)

2 eggs

1 tsp vanilla extract

½ cup (50 g) almond flour

⅓ cup (40 g) coconut flour

⅓ cup (40 g) cacao powder

2 tbsp (24 g) coconut sugar

½ tsp baking powder

½ tsp baking soda

¼ tsp salt

½ cup (90 g) dairy-free chocolate chips (optional, I prefer Enjoy Life brand)

½ cup (75 g) chopped walnuts (optional)

In a large bowl, mix the bananas, eggs and vanilla until smooth.

In a separate bowl, combine the flours, cacao powder, sugar, baking powder, baking soda and salt. Fold into the banana mixture. Mix together until just combined, being careful not to overmix. If desired, fold in the chocolate chips, reserving a few for garnish, and the walnuts.

Line a 3- to 4-quart (2.7- to 3.6-L) slow cooker with parchment paper and then use a spatula to pour the batter into the slow cooker and spread evenly. Sprinkle the reserved chocolate chips on top of the batter, line the slow cooker lid with a few paper towels to absorb the moisture and cover.

Cook on low for 4 hours or on high for 2 hours, or until a toothpick inserted into the center comes out clean. Remove from the slow cooker using the parchment paper and let cool. Slice and enjoy within 7 days, or freeze for up to 3 months.

COOKING TIP:

- *Use chip clips to hold the parchment paper in place by clipping it to the sides while you're pouring in the batter.*

Per serving: Calories: 130 | Fat: 4.5 g | Carbs: 18.1 g | Fiber: 3.3 g | Protein: 4.7 g

PALEO-PERFECT PEAR CRISP

This is a simple, healthy dessert that no one will even know is free of refined sugar and grains. One of my friends, who's against all things nuts as replacements, said that once the crumble was crumbled, she couldn't even tell the difference! Top with some coconut whipped cream and dig in! Double this recipe using a 6-quart (5.4-L) slow cooker for 8 servings.

PEAR FILLING

4 cups (600 g) peeled, cored and diced or sliced Bartlett or Bosc pears (about 3 medium)

1½ tsp (8 ml) lemon juice (optional, to prevent browning)

3 tbsp (36 g) coconut sugar

1 tbsp (8 g) arrowroot flour

1 tsp vanilla extract

½ tsp ground cinnamon

¼ tsp ground nutmeg

TOPPING

1 cup (150 g) raw pecans or walnuts

½ cup (50 g) blanched almond flour

2 tbsp (30 ml) ghee, homemade (page 180) or store-bought, or coconut oil, melted

2 tbsp (30 ml) maple syrup

½ tsp ground ginger

¼ tsp salt

To make the pear filling, combine the pears, lemon juice (if using), sugar, flour, vanilla, cinnamon and nutmeg in a 3-quart (2.7-L) slow cooker and stir to evenly coat the pears.

To make the topping, crush the pecans until small and crumbly. Pecans are fairly soft and while you could do this in a food processor, a simple way to crush them is to place the nuts on a cutting board or into a paper or plastic bag and gently hammer with a flat-bottomed measuring cup, meat mallet or rolling pin.

Combine the crushed pecans, almond flour, ghee, maple syrup, ginger and salt in a bowl and stir until the mixture is sticky. Evenly spread the topping over the pears. Cover and cook on low for 3 to 4 hours or on high for 1 to 2 hours, or until the pears are soft and appear caramelized.

Crisps are best eaten the same day but can be kept covered for up to 3 days in the refrigerator. Baked fruit crisps can be frozen for up to 3 months. Allow to cool completely and freeze in an airtight container. To reheat, thaw in the refrigerator and then bake in a 375°F (190°C) oven for 20 minutes, or until warmed through.

COOKING TIP:

- *Change it up and replace 2 cups (300 g) of the pears with 2 cups (240 g) of cranberries or 2 cups (300 g) of peeled and diced apple.*

- *Replace ghee with coconut oil to make this vegan.*

Per serving: Calories: 281 | Fat: 19.5 g | Carbs: 28 g | Fiber: 5.2 g | Protein: 2.3 g

PUMPKIN BARS WITH MAPLE FROSTING

VEGETARIAN

While these Paleo pumpkin bars are perfect for fall baking, you don't need it to be autumn to make these. They really are a wonderful (and healthy!) treat any time of the year, and you'll love that they're easy to throw together and "bake" while you run errands. There's no guilt with these cookie bars—only deliciousness you'll feel good about eating!

MAKES 8 BARS

PUMPKIN BARS

1 cup (100 g) fine blanched almond flour (not almond meal)

¼ cup (25 g) coconut flour

⅔ cup (120 g) coconut sugar

1½ tsp (5 g) pumpkin pie spice

2 tsp (6 g) ground cinnamon

1 tsp ground ginger

½ tsp baking soda

¼ tsp salt

1 whole egg plus 1 yolk

⅔ cup (170 g) pumpkin puree

¼ cup (65 g) smooth almond butter

1½ tsp (8 ml) vanilla extract

MAPLE FROSTING

½ cup (120 ml) coconut oil

⅓ cup (80 ml) maple syrup

2 tbsp (30 ml) ghee, homemade (page 180) or store-bought

2 tbsp (30 ml) almond milk

½ tsp vanilla extract

To make the pumpkin bars, combine the flours, sugar, pumpkin pie spice, cinnamon, ginger, baking soda and salt in a large bowl. Add the egg, egg yolk, pumpkin puree, almond butter and vanilla. Mix well to combine.

Line a 3- to 4-quart (2.7- to 3.6-L) slow cooker with parchment paper and then use a spatula to pour the mixture into the slow cooker and spread evenly. Place a layer of paper towels just beneath the slow cooker lid to collect the condensation. Cover and cook on low for 3 hours or on high for 1 to 1½ hours. Remove from the slow cooker using the corners of the parchment paper and let cool.

To make the frosting, place the coconut oil, maple syrup and ghee in a microwave-safe bowl and cook in 30-second increments until softened. Add the almond milk and vanilla and use a hand mixer or an immersion blender to beat until fluffy, 3 to 4 minutes.

Use an offset spatula to spread the frosting in an even layer and then cut into wedges.

COOKING TIP:

- *Use chip clips to hold the parchment paper in place by clipping it to the sides of the insert while you're pouring in the batter.*

Per serving: Calories: 382 | Fat: 25.3 g | Carbs: 33.5 g | Fiber: 4.8 g | Protein: 7.6 g

Simplified Paleo
STAPLES

These Paleo staples are things that will make your day-to-day Paleo life easier and more affordable. By making your own sauces, salsas and broths, you'll always have them on hand and you'll be able to feed yourself and your loved ones additive-free, sugar-free, junk-free options that can be hard (or expensive) to find out in the wild.

I almost always have homemade marinara (page 179) frozen in 2-cup (480-ml) portions in my freezer for simple weeknight dinners, and I can't even tell you how much money I've saved by making my own beef and chicken broths (page 183). To make the deal even sweeter, they're all made in the slow cooker, so you have less work, fewer dishes and less hassle to get these real-food options in your hands.

RESTAURANT RED SALSA

This salsa is great for entertaining, enjoying at BBQs, game day parties or taco night or for using up all of those tomatoes from your garden's summer harvest. It's easily customizable to anyone's desired spice level, and I love keeping it in 1-cup (240-ml) containers in the freezer to bring together easy meals like fajita bowls (page 124) or when guests are coming over.

**MAKES
2–3 CUPS (480–720 ML)**

8 plum tomatoes, cored and quartered (about 1½ lb [680 g])

1 large white onion, quartered

1 large red onion, quartered

1 red bell pepper, cored and quartered

1 tbsp (10 g) minced garlic

1 tsp salt

1 tsp chili powder

1 tsp cumin

½ cup (65 g) diced jalapeño, seeded (about 2)

1 cup (30 g) cilantro leaves

Place the tomatoes, onions, bell pepper, garlic, salt, chili powder, cumin and jalapeño in the slow cooker. Cover and cook on low for 4 to 6 hours or on high for 2 to 3 hours.

You can choose to vent the slow cooker by tilting the lid slightly and cooking an additional 1 hour to slightly brown the vegetables and remove excess liquid, which will yield a thicker salsa with a more roasted flavor.

Once the vegetables are completely softened and easily mashable with a fork, add the cilantro and then blend with an immersion blender, or transfer to a food processor and pulse to combine until the salsa is the desired texture. Chill for 1 to 2 hours before serving.

Place in an airtight container to store in the refrigerator for 7 to 10 days, or in the freezer for up to 3 months.

COOKING TIP:

- *Jalapeño seeds are the source of the pepper's heat, and these can be kept in for a hotter salsa or completely removed for a mild salsa.*

Per ¼-cup (60-g) serving: Calories: 25 | Fat: 0.01 g | Carbs: 5.1 g | Fiber: 1.5 g | Protein: 1.2 g

HOMEMADE KETCHUP

I've found the trick to getting my husband Justin to eat anything is to ensure he can cover it liberally in ketchup. It's a real refined palate he has, isn't it? But hey, it helps him get healthier, dairy-free, gluten-free foods on his plate, so I'm not complaining. And with this slow cooker recipe, there's really nothing to complain about because it's just so dang easy.

MAKES 2–3 CUPS (470–700 G)

1 (28-oz [784-g] can) crushed tomatoes

½ cup (90 g) chopped pitted Medjool dates or ¼ cup (60 ml) honey

¼ cup (60 ml) apple cider vinegar

1 tsp garlic powder

1 tsp onion powder

1 tsp salt

1 tsp paprika

⅛ tsp allspice

Add the tomatoes, dates, vinegar, garlic powder, onion powder, salt, paprika and allspice to the slow cooker. Cover and cook on high for 3 to 4 hours or on low for 6 to 7 hours, until the ketchup has thickened and reduced.

Use an immersion blender to puree until it's a smooth consistency, or transfer to a blender or food processor. Let the ketchup cool, and then refrigerate in an airtight container for up to 5 days, or freeze in a freezer-safe container for up to 4 months. You can also freeze the ketchup first in an ice cube tray and then transfer to a freezer-safe bag for smaller amounts when needed.

COOKING TIP:

- *Slightly tilt the slow cooker lid so there is an opening to let the steam escape during the last 30 minutes if the ketchup looks too watery.*

Per 2-tbsp (30-g) serving: Calories: 22 | Fat: 0 g | Carbs: 5.2 g | Fiber: 0.9 g | Protein: 0.7 g

EASY PEASY BBQ SAUCE

If you've ever wanted to make homemade BBQ sauce, but found it a little too fussy for your taste, the slow cooker is about to change that. Short of measuring the ingredients for you, it takes care of all the heavy lifting, producing a deep, vibrant sauce that's like nothing you'll ever taste from the grocery store.

MAKES 3 CUPS (700 G)

1 (14-oz [392-g]) can tomato sauce

1 (6-oz [168-g]) can tomato paste

1 cup (240 ml) unsweetened apple juice

⅓ cup (80 ml) water

¼ cup (60 ml) apple cider vinegar or balsamic vinegar

1 tbsp (15 g) Dijon mustard

1½ tsp (4 g) smoked paprika

1 tsp salt

1 tsp garlic powder

1 tsp onion powder

½ tsp cayenne pepper

6 dates, pitted and chopped (optional)

1–2 tsp liquid smoke (optional, I prefer Wright's or Cedar House)

Add the tomato sauce, tomato paste, juice, water, vinegar, mustard, paprika, salt, garlic powder, onion powder, cayenne, dates (if using) and liquid smoke to taste (if using) to the slow cooker and stir well to combine. Cook on low for 4 to 6 hours or on high for 2 to 3 hours.

Use an immersion blender to blend in the slow cooker, or transfer to a food processor or blender and blend until smooth.

Let cool and store in an airtight container in the fridge for up to 10 days, or in the freezer for up to 3 months.

Per 2-tbsp (30-g) serving: Calories: 50 | Fat: 0.2 g | Carbs: 18 g | Fiber: 4 g | Protein 1.2 g

DIY MARINARA AND PIZZA SAUCE

VEGAN OPTION · LOW-CARB · FREEZER FRIENDLY · NUT-FREE · EGG-FREE

This recipe is one that I've memorized after years of helping with the summer tomato harvest. It's the perfect way to use up extra produce, or to make and freeze your own budget-friendly, additive- and sugar-free sauce. Roma or San Marzano tomatoes are ideal for homemade marinara. These are firmer, meatier and on the smaller side and make for a thick, rich-tasting sauce.

> **MAKES 6 CUPS (1.4 KG) MARINARA, 1 SCANT CUP (235 ML) PIZZA SAUCE**

DIY MARINARA

5–6 lb (2.3–2.7 kg) paste tomatoes or 2 (28-oz [784-g]) cans crushed tomatoes

4 cloves garlic, crushed

1 (6-oz [168-g]) can tomato paste

1 medium white onion, diced

1 tbsp (15 ml) extra virgin olive oil

¼ cup (60 ml) 100% cranberry or pomegranate juice (optional)

1 tbsp (3 g) dried parsley

2 tsp (2 g) dried basil

1 tsp dried oregano

1 tsp dried thyme

1 tsp salt, plus more to taste

½ tsp ground black pepper, plus more to taste

1 bay leaf

PIZZA SAUCE

½ cup (120 ml) DIY Marinara

2 tbsp (6 g) dried basil

2 tbsp (6 g) dried oregano

1 tbsp (3 g) dried minced garlic

1 tbsp (2 g) dried onion flakes

1 tbsp (3 g) dried parsley

1 tsp fennel seeds

1 tsp dried thyme

½ tsp salt

To make the marinara, add the tomatoes, garlic, tomato paste, onion, oil, juice (if using), parsley, basil, oregano, thyme, salt, pepper and bay leaf to the slow cooker. Cover and cook on low for 3 to 4 hours. Remove the bay leaf.

With an immersion blender or food processor, blend the vegetables until they're a smooth consistency. Add salt and pepper to taste then transfer to glass jars and allow to cool before putting on the lids. Store in the refrigerator in an airtight container for up to 5 days, or freeze in a freezer-safe container for up to 4 months.

To make the pizza sauce, in a bowl, combine the marinara, basil, oregano, garlic, onion flakes, parsley, fennel seeds, thyme and salt. Serve immediately, or store for up to 7 days in the refrigerator.

COOKING TIPS:

- *You can strain the marinara through a fine-mesh strainer to remove any remaining seeds after blending if you prefer a really smooth sauce. To thicken the sauce further, you can return it to the slow cooker after straining and cook with the lid vented for an additional 1 to 2 hours on low.*

- *Once you get the hang of making your own sauce, start experimenting with different spice combinations: ramp up the garlic for a garlic marinara, create a spicy red pepper marinara or add 2 cups (140 g) of diced mushrooms during the last hour of cooking for a mushroom marinara.*

Marinara sauce (per ¼-cup [60-g] serving): Calories: 60 | Fat: 1.2 g | Carbs: 10 g | Fiber: 2.5 g | Protein: 1.9 g

Pizza sauce (per ¼-cup [60-g] serving): Calories: 62 | Fat: 1.2 g | Carbs: 10 g | Fiber: 2.5 g | Protein: 1.9 g

SKIP-THE-STORE
SLOW COOKER GHEE

Ghee is a great staple for a Paleo diet because it offers quality fats and a rich butter flavor but without the dairy or the price tag of more expensive options. This ghee recipe is made easily in a slow cooker and can be stored for long periods of time. Homemade ghee is one of my favorite fats to use for sautéing vegetables, scrambling eggs, stirring into veggie mash, using in shrimp scampi or dolloping on steak.

MAKES 12 OZ (340 G)

16 oz (455 g) unsalted butter, such as Kerrygold

Place the butter in the slow cooker and cover with the lid. Cook on low for 2 to 3 hours, or until the milk solids fall to the bottom of the pot and turn brown; do not stir during cooking.

Place a double layer of cheesecloth over the mouth of a storage jar (wide-mouth Mason or Weck glass jars work best). Carefully pour the liquid from the slow cooker into the jar through the cheesecloth (use a funnel, measuring cup with a spout or even a large baster). The milk solids will accumulate on top of the cheesecloth. Use a new piece of cheesecloth if it gets too clogged. Discard the milk solids.

Let the ghee cool for about an hour, then seal with a lid. Store in a cabinet away from the light for up to 3 months, or in the refrigerator for up to a year.

Per 2-tbsp (30-g) serving: Calories: 100 | Fat: 12 g | Carbs: 0 g | Fiber: 0 g | Protein: 0 g

BETTER-THAN-BOXED BEEF OR CHICKEN BROTH

FREEZER FRIENDLY · AIP FRIENDLY · NUT-FREE · EGG-FREE · LOW-CARB

MAKES 3 QUARTS (2.7 L)

I remember the shock in my grandma's voice as she yelled, "You're throwing away the best parts!" when she saw me tossing cooked bones right into the trash. I got a valuable lesson that day on why making your own broth is not only more economical, but more nutritious too. When I started making it on my own consistently, I was really surprised at just how easy it is to do. Making it in the slow cooker is always the way to go for me, as it means I don't have to leave my gas stove on for 12+ hours, and I can just let the slow cooker do its thing!

1 (4–5-lb [1.8–2.3-kg]) chicken carcass or the equivalent in chicken bones, or approximately 3 lb (1.4 kg) beef bones

1 large onion, roughly chopped

3–4 celery ribs or the trimmed ends of 2 heads celery

3 carrots, roughly chopped into large pieces

Large handful of fresh herbs (such as parsley, rosemary or thyme)

1 tsp ground black pepper

2 bay leaves

2 cloves garlic, cut in half

Add the bones, onion, celery, carrots, herbs, pepper, bay leaves and garlic to the slow cooker and then fill it two-thirds with water. Cook on low for 8 to 10 hours.

Remove and discard the bones, large vegetables and bay leaves. Pour the broth through a mesh strainer into a large bowl. Transfer the broth to airtight containers, and let the broth cool to room temperature prior to storing. You can skim off the fat from the top once it's cooled if you prefer. Store in the refrigerator for up to 5 days, or freeze in freezer-safe containers for up to 3 months.

COOKING TIP:

- I have learned to omit salt from my broth when I make it, and to instead add it when I'm using it. This prevents a recipe that calls for broth and salt from becoming too salty. However, you can add salt to your own broth per your preference.

Per 1-cup (240-ml) serving: Calories: 20 | Fat: 2 g | Carbs: 0 g | Fiber: 0 g | Protein: 6 g

ACKNOWLEDGMENTS, HUGS AND HIGH FIVES

For my nana, my biggest fan from the start. Thank you for always supporting me marching to the beat of my own drum all of these years and trusting that I'd make it onto the path that was right for me. Thank you for making me feel like I'm the smartest, most capable, most talented person whenever I'm near you. You're the best at being my nana.

To Alex, for the constant, unwavering sisterhood that's helped me find my way through this world over the last twenty years. For decades of being my first call for the hard stuff and the happy stuff. For bringing out the best in me, even when you have to yank it. For sometimes being our strength that's pushing me through first and sometimes being our guiding light leading the way. We make the best team for two people so terrible at sports.

To Dad and Poppy, the two most creative and artistic people I know. I'm so grateful to have inherited even just a bit of that genetic code from you both. Thank you for being so dang talented and inspiring me endlessly. While it's not a pirate bust or a coffee table, this book is an absolute reflection of what you've imparted to me. I love you both.

To Uncle Mike: When I was eight and we were ice fishing, you gave me the first of many pieces of business advice I'd never forget. Two decades and a lot of words of wisdom later, you are right. About all of it. Your guidance over the years has shaped my life into my dream life. And Auntie Mandy, who gave to me freely, and never asked questions or asked for anything in return. Everything you've done for me and taught me has been a stepping stone to here.

To my mom: Thank you for instilling your work ethic in me and making the sacrifices you did for me. Thank you for raising me to believe I can do anything in this life. Look, Ma, I did it! You did a great job, and this book is just as much your accomplishment as it is mine. I love you.

To Auntie Kim: Thank you for always believing in me and supporting me, even when it was hard. You are the example of selflessness that I aspire to be, the kick in the pants when I need it and the reminder that life is what I make of it. I'm grateful for you beyond measure. Thank you for never giving up on me.

To Jen and Janelle, the best of the best. Somehow, you're not sick of me yet, and for that I am grateful. Thank you for keeping me sane these many years, and mostly, thank you for loving me long before I knew I was worth loving myself. There are legitimately no words for how much I love you. It's just too much.

To Cristina and Kyndra: Your creativity, strength and work ethic inspire mine, and your friendship pushes me to continually raise the bar, both personally and professionally, on loving with intention and living with integrity. You are the people you surround yourself with, and it is one of my greatest gifts to be surrounded by you.

To Caitlin, Meg and the incredible, talented team at Page Street: Thank you for seeing something in me and giving me the opportunity to do what I love. Your help (lots of it), patience (unending amounts) and support (so much of it) have meant everything. Thank you for turning one girl's dream into the best reality. All of the hugs.

To Shanna, Melissa, Jen, Steph and the entire Whole30 team: Thank you for the opportunities you've given me, the doors you've opened and the countless ways you've lifted my voice. I am thankful for the way your individual talents, strengths and compassion have enriched my life both personally and professionally.

To Anna and Mark: You are the best. Thank you. You were two of the first to believe in me.

And for Justin, again, because this year was a long one for you, too. The number of dishes you did, the long days and nights you stayed up with me while I worked and the almost daily trips to the grocery store you took for months on end to help make my dream come true are nothing short of selfless acts of love and partnership. For eating leftovers (and overs again) as I tested and adjusted, and for assuring me the recipes are good, the book is good and I am good. This life is best lived with you by my side. And, finally, thank you for always making me coffee.

And to my Whole Kitchen Sink readers, my fellow creators and my incredible community that allows me to be a part of their lives: This cookbook is for you. Your encouragement, support and trust make me want to be a better human in all ways. None of this is possible without you. I'll continue to work to help you change your life as thanks for how you've changed mine. You have my deepest gratitude, forever. You'll always have a seat at my table.

ABOUT THE AUTHOR

Bailey Fischer is the creator and writer behind the successful food and wellness website Whole Kitchen Sink. Born from a need to teach herself to cook real food that tastes good, in ways that didn't stress her limited time or budget, her website is dedicated to helping others find health and healing using what she's learned.

After growing up overweight and reaching 290 pounds (132 kg) at twenty-two years old, she has now transformed her entire life and believes that real food truly does heal, and that it doesn't have to be complicated. Her recipes and writing have been published in *Paleo Magazine*, Whole30.com, BuzzFeed, Mark's Daily Apple, *Clean Eating Magazine* and more.

When she's not writing or creating real-food recipes, you can find her traveling the world with her husband or hanging with her rescue pups, Olivia and Charlie, around Minneapolis, Minnesota, where they happily reside.